HUMAN ETERNITY : STONE AGE TO MUSTOPIA

By the same author

1. Conflicts and Co-existence – India
2. Development of the Resources of the Sea: India
3. Religion and Philosophy for Modern Youth
4. Bengal: The Unique State

About the Author

Prof. J.N. Nanda, with a string of academic distinctions including two earned doctorates, multitude of awards from the IBC and American Biography Association, and other national and international awards, is a distinguished scientist, thinker and writer. He has represented India abroad many times. He has summarized his all embracing philosophy and religion as New Mahayana in which all 'isms' co-exist. Among his scientific contributions, mention can be made of his new light on the earth's internal structure, the origin of the moon and the origin of earth's magnetism etc. He has travelled practically in all continents and studied many languages. Besides his scientific books and publications, mention may be made of his book "Science and Technology in India's Transformation", released by the President of India at the Rashtrapati Bhawan in 1986. Other important books are *Foreign Policy of Co-existence– India, Glimpses of Indian History and Culture,* and *Co-operative Development of Marine Resources.*

HUMAN ETERNITY
Stone Age to Mustopia

By
J.N. NANDA

CONCEPT PUBLISHING COMPANY, NEW DELHI-110059

Cataloging in Publication Data—DK
Courtesy: D.K. Agencies (P) Ltd. <docinfo@dkagencies.com>

Nanda, J. N. (Jatinder Nath), 1920-
Human eternity : stone age to mustopia / by J.N. Nanda.
p. cm.
Includes bibliographical references (p.
Includes index.
ISBN 8180693333

1. Civilization—History. I. Title.

DDC 909 22

ISBN 81-8069-333-3

First Published 2006

Published and Printed by
Ashok Kumar Mittal
Concept Publishing Company
A/15-16, Commercial Block, Mohan Garden,
New Delhi-110059 (India)

Phones: 25351460, 25351794
Fax: 091-(11)-25357103
Email : publishing@conceptpub.com

FOREWORD

Prof. J.N. Nanda has drawn timely attention of all humanity to the dire need of closing ranks against rampant disease of corruption and violence since once these last obstacles are overcome, sky is the limit for the advancement of civilization and human happiness. One has to be conscious of the immense time still available to human eternity of one or two billion years of continuous progress and increase in well-being. The time of planning for Mustopia (oughtopia of Young of Korea) is only now when nationalism is giving way to internationalism and governance led by U.N. and the U.N. itself is poised to undergo democratic reform. He has suggested a fairly acceptable alternative to veto in the Security Council.

The only blocks in human progress and smooth march of civilization are corruption and terrorism. His suggestions to speedily overcome these are worth acceptance. Nations may have to learn some lessons in utilizing force of innocent children from the leaders (later discarded) of the cultural revolution in China. The device of democratic inter-governmental conferences has been successfully used to discover commonality of interest and requirement of an international regime of the law of the sea. Similar transparent diplomatic skills should be employed in discussing reform in all religions. Such problems can be solved within a century or two and the world can have more resources for increasing human happiness all over the world. Among the new axioms of life will be established, regard for universal human rights and a climate of human brotherhood and mutual esteem. The world is alerted to the possibility of billions of years for human progress or human destruction through the ill dreamt selfish progress of a few at the cost of others and incessant see-saw struggles for upmanship.

Prof. Nanda has often given instances from the environment in India, a mini-cosmos and a believer in unity in diversity and coexistence of all faiths and isms. It promises to never have aggressive ambitions against any group or minority within the country or any other nation. He is certain that the Indian approach will be successful and this kindles a hope for world of peace and co-operation. The nations are going through the initial phase of governance by UN system. Many international concerns are now managed under the leadership of UN agencies or similar world bodies. A little more effort is now in order for codifying the international law and for setting up an international police force and world courts. The strange new findings in molecular biology, human nudging of evolutionary processes and further insight into working of the mind would bring about a climate of acceptance and discarding of attitudes of confrontation. We are on the verge of discovering how new thoughts arise and the nature of intuition.

The author has summarized, in a few pages, the history of civilization so far assigning all progress to the genius of few gifted individuals. The serious onward march has begun with the discovery of the scientific method and of democracy as the engine of welfare of all.

Dr. A.R. Kidwai

AUTHOR'S PREFACE

This book deals with the history of wars, apostles of peace, dictators and emperors. We have had the advantage of many persons of genius and ingenuity. There has been a spurt of inventions, innovations and new technologies. Strides have been made towards a global organization of mankind not simply for trade and commerce but for universal increase of wealth and happiness. We are building a world for unity in diversity and the whole world to act as a single family. The goal is remunerative work for everyone, guaranteed subsistence allowance for every person: man, woman and child. An uplifting education, value maintaining entertainment and leisure activities are to be made available.

Eternity of people is the history and adventure of mankind from hoary antiquity to far into the future when the earth might end as a habitat for mankind. The past is naturally what we know about. The future is unknown except what can be expected to happen by extrapolation from the past and from the purposeful actions of mankind. Man is the only creature, who can think and plan for the best possible future and take steps to cease being a plaything of fate, uncontrolled environment and well-known enemies residing in his own brain like laziness, anger, suspicion, greed, etc. He has been learning from thousands of past teachers and gurus. He has already made advances in science and technology. He has practically achieved rule of law in the world. Wars are no longer options for unstable nations. Globalization of trade and commerce is reaching everywhere. United Nations has been established. There is a single super power which is a firm advocate of UN and believes that a reformed constitution can make it more democratic and acceptable to the whole of mankind. The law of reforms and progress has been discovered i.e. by discussion, democratic mechanisms and convincing of people without coercion. Defence of society has to be carried out by all means and the UN will be active in setting up arrangements for internal and external defence of all nations. Now is the time to assure ourselves that the world will continue to develop in the common interest and to introduce new education and economics that will assure eradication of want and poverty, security of self and insurance against want. Democracy, assured human rights and mutual regard and assistance can build a heaven on earth for mankind to enjoy till eternity which will go far into the future.

The goal is to have a guaranteed subsistence allowance for all adults and at least one dependent for each. The new society will provide an uplifting education and value based leisure activities for everyone. Man's greatest enemy has been man. Man is the chief polluting agent of the environment. He has used the resources without thought for their replacement or for sustainable development or for a concern for leaving a legacy of poverty and ignorance for the future generations. A rebuilding of society for peaceful and purposeful existence is to be started. Man has to be an embodiment of freedom, friendship, loyalty and creativity. The recipe for continuous healthy and busy existence on earth is love and ability.

Young Seek Choue of Korea presented his Oughtopia Peace Model at the 22nd International Day of Peace in 1983. We are replacing "ought" by "must" or a planned certainty as the time unfolds its approaching millennia of purposeful development. Any lacunae in national or international law will be set right by universal democratic agreement. All national cooperating states will be the framework for future governance. The accent will be on "unity in diversity".

The author is indebted to Shri Manohar Singh Batra for looking over the manuscript and suggesting some improvements. He is also thankful to his family for support and looking up the internet when requested. He is grateful to H.E. Dr. A.R. Kidwai, for agreeing to write a foreword for this book and for many valuable suggestions.

CONTENTS

1

INTRODUCTION

The dimension of time has been truncated since it was recognized that it has no significance in the absence of a universe. It is now common belief that the universe had a big bang beginning when time also started. Time does not start from some instant-minus infinity – but from an instant, a few billion years before the present. Will the time go on elapsing after the universe vanishes in a gigantic black hole? According to the current thinking that instant would be the future end point of time. For the people, the eternity begins when human gene made an evolving monkey walk on two legs and he/she gave evidence of a thinking mind. His eternity will end when his habitat that is the earth can no longer support him. Possibly the sun fails by turning into a collapsing star or when all planets enter a disorderly mode. The eternity of human beings can be shortened in the past to the distant time when the first inspired human taught rules of conduct, be it in sacred sayings that later were written down after the invention of writing and reading. This could be around 3000 years before Christ. The future would be restricted to millions of years hence unless by own folly man makes the earth barren of life. We wish to examine the past and the future of human existence. The only road block of future by irony of nature would be another ice-age.

Eternity for any individual is limited to his span of life. People desired to live longer than the limited life span of their body. This led to two distinct ways of solving the issue. One led to the mummification or burial in long lasting structures like the pyramids of Egypt or well guarded tombs of China often by terra cotta soldiers tier upon tier. The other way was more a mental construct and it chiefly operated in India. The people en masse were mesmerized into the belief that an individual was not just the living body but he was body till it lasted as well as a soul that was ever lasting. Simplest description of the soul was that it was a part of the essence of all pervading cosmic existence and consciousness usually christened God. The second proposition that went along with the belief in soul was a belief in the transmigration of soul and rebirth. Certain scriptures regarded individual eternity to be an eternity in heaven or hell after the judgement day, when God assigns souls according to their deeds in the physical life on earth. The Hindus who had advanced the idea of soul regarded it to be eternally involved in a cycle of births and rebirths. The cycle could be broken if an individual in a human incarnation lived a life of virtue and being busy in the welfare of others. The chief virtues were truth, non-violence and selfless service. The break in the cycle of births was termed Buddhahood or reaching Moksha in Hinduism or salvation or liberation in other philosophies. The eternity for the individual in such beliefs would extend to an expected point of salvation. Each individual was to make efforts to cut this period as short as he could. The Hindus were always very practical minded and assured any Hindu that he could reach salvation by a short cut by bathing in the Ganges or many similar sacred waters or through love of God or fellow man.

In this book, we will not be dealing with the eternity of an identifiable human being, but of humanity as a whole. A human being can also be supposed to be in a limited sense eternal when his ancestors and descendents are taken into view. This eternity is coincidental with the biosphere from its start to its end. The real danger to man is from himself. Life may be throttled by ever increasing pollution or internecine rioting and warfare.

To ensure continuation of life, man has to build a world of tolerance, mutual acceptance and respect for the rights of all. The danger to humanity exists still from the occurrence of natural calamities like a vast deluge, a devastating spread of fire, the rising of the surface of the oceans a few meters, the freezing again of water in large glaciers, or the temperature suddenly rising or falling. These have little likelihood and human skills have advanced sufficiently for protecting him in pockets of time or space allowing a fresh continuation. Continued scientific and technological competence will determine the eternity of human being on earth or in the cosmos in case man learns space travel and builds colonies under different skies, a projection of the discovery of the new world in the 15th century for the distant future.

Human resource development refers to the development of the production skills. Human development is concerned with the health, toughness and inter-personal skills of the individual. After graduating from school, every child should enter a two year human development course learning discipline and healthy routine and broad education in history and literature. After this kind of enlistment, the child can opt for a three year university or technology degree course in a field of his choice including education, agriculture, engineering, science, management, commerce, emerging technologies and others fields. During this university degree course, basic knowledge of mathematics, electronics and an international language will also be included. Some of the learning may have to be accomplished in the school vacations or in the enlistment period of two years already provided. Toppers in all areas will be encouraged by lucrative stipends to go for advanced study and research. All students will be attached to science and technology establishment, professional internships or first entry service in governance or in management. Children and youth will be welcome to earn extra pocket money by part time employment and such project experience will count to the credit of the child during his schooling. There will be exposure to music and fine arts and a gifted child will be admitted to an appropriate teacher or teachers for lifetime. Everyone will be instructed in Brahmacharya (celibacy outside marriage) and in Yogic exercises and meditation. People will take to work culture and accept special rewards for those who demonstrate merit and sustained hard work in all fields including sports, swimming and other outdoor activities and social work. A sincere regard for human rights of all will be instilled. The youth will learn that love and friendship are exalted over all other attitudes as mankind can progress unitedly only through love and friendship, the global ideal is contained in the Indian saying that the whole mankind is but one family and the ideal man is one who feels the pain of others.

In the past, the trade was carried on like farming, at subsistence level. Now the globalization of trade and commerce has been attempted under the auspices of big money. There is free flow of goods and capital. The large corporations have outlets and godowns in many countries. All nations are voluntarily participating in the global activity in their own interest for increase in prosperity and useful friendships. Any hardship caused to certain workers in industries that are less competitive than imports from more successful companies abroad, is compensated by facilities for retraining or by payment of adjustment funds. The economic indices show more prosperity with larger trade and commerce. The indirect advantages of people to people contacts and knowledge of insurance and honest dealings are also of great value. Multinational corporations will increase the usual transfer of wealth and know-how for industrial and organizational advance; computer being in the saddle everywhere. Within the next couple of centuries, if global peace lasts, the entire world will become closely knit in farsighted human international collaborations. The former utopias as proposed by Plato or Thomas More and others (Marx or Rousseau) were limited in scope to a single and exclusive ideology accepted by few close followers. The global culture now being built is for the entire population of the world excluding none. The ideology is of unity in diversity, a culture of fellow feeling and friendship to all. It will be global common society taking ever new steps to promote peace and friendship. Urbanization, friendly to people and environment, will spread. The decision making will be by participative democracy avoiding massification. The individual incomes will push all above poverty line or the incomes will guarantee reasonable and comfortable living standards as well as self-actualization to all. Means will be found to cope with the variation in human beliefs by open discussion and acceptance of differences as well as the evolutionary changes in any one's views. A system of global governance consistent with human rights will emerge from UN efforts. The "Mustopia" will be a certainty after a few centuries of united effort.

2

EARLY STIRRINGS

The earth when put together from the debris of an exploded star was initially a liquid mass possibly with a thin solidified crust. An atmosphere of poisonous gases or nitrogen rose from inside the earth. There were sudden convulsions due to chemical changes and after about seven hundred million years, close to the centre of the earth, on account of gravitational separation at the surface of a central uranium sphere, a fissionable layer of isotope of atomic weight 235 of uranium was formed. The energy released in the explosion was responsible for the explosive emission of a large mass from the earth which caused the earth to tilt by 12.2 degrees. Large part of the emitted mass fell back to the earth but some mass including a thick slab of iron began to orbit around the earth at a distance beyond 2.5 times the radius of the earth. This became the core of the moon which grew in size and also kept moving away from the earth. The upheaval inside the earth released enormous quantities of water and large ocean appeared all over the globe. A bacteria appeared that released oxygen from the carbonates in the rocks. With the occurrence of oxygen, the biological cells that need oxygen came into being and the long road of creative biology was begun. For two billion years of earth's existence, the scene was utterly barren and not a blade of grass grew; two billion years after the first explosion, there is evidence that a second explosion in the earth took place. Besides the earth getting more tilted to the present 23.4 degrees, there was no release of the core of a second moon. The stage was finally set for the evolution of genes and bio-molecules. Creative evolution was at work in the plant as well as marine biota. The biological history painfully put together by the geologists goes back only to the four to five hundred million years and human beings evolved only few hundred thousand years ago. For most of this time they worked hard to achieve elementary knowledge useful for collecting forest produce or for catching fish or for hunting some animals. In the last hundred thousands years they were already supporting themselves in tribal groups, living in caves and such shelters and embarking on the discovery of the secret of growing plants and grain or taming some animals like sheep and cows and had learnt the art and science of building a fire and started cooking their food and learnt the location of salt rocks or of salt in some patches near the coast. The first barter began with trade for salt. Indians and Arab-Africans around the Red Sea had a head start in this trade. Soon river and coastal trade and travel in rafts and junks or boats began.

Thus stone age had arrived. They had only stone implements but accomplished wonders with back-breaking labour and love of their gods in the heart. They learnt the use of fire and later of the wheel and the pulley. Throwing sticks were invented to help in hunting. Mogli of the movies still uses these. Australia's natives have these as a recognition symbol. The creative evolution was busy in evolving wild rice, wheat and lotus flowers and seeds. The plant varieties, birds via carnivorous and vegetarian giant lizards and dragons, and variety of animals appeared. Man flexed his muscles and brain to understand and collect seeds and grow grains and fruit. As a part of agricultural advance the taming of sheep and cows provided the luxury of ready supply of food and milk. From the drawings that survive till now in the ancient cave shelters or on rooks, one can state with certainty that even the primitive man had a sensitivity for line and form. Such drawings are to be seen in Europe, India and possibly in other countries. In India some easily accessible cave paintings exist in the Bhima caves near Bhopal. Life must have been very hard. People were afraid to meet strangers. Property was held in common as tribal property for use of all. This is practically still prevalent on the Easter Island. Neanderthal man, 50000 years ago buried customary gifts with the burials. The idea of private property came much later when there was more stuff and more order. Tribal communes and later in India self-sufficient village co-operatives were established allowing private farms and private property but there was customary co-operative labour. Money appeared much later and in India village economy was run by directly using labour bartered for grain or food. The potter and weaver was the value adding technologist and most villages were self sufficient in pottery artifacts, woven cotton cloth or wool or woven reeds as mats and thatch. A professional caste system was natural since all instruction was in the family day-to-day work. The system of co-operation and natural warmth of human companionship made government almost unnecessary. The goal of communism of banishing the state from society was almost achieved at start. Latter it became almost impossible for so many chores got being progressively assigned to the state. From the very start families began to be led by the eldest in the family and paternal or maternal organization of society began.

The tropical and temperate forests were almost impassable and the few families and small tribes living in these could easily subsist on forest berries, roots and fish in the rivers and ponds. They had no challenging tasks and were happily subsisting. Even now primitives in the Andamans and Nicobars, in Greenland, or with the natives of Australia and eastern Himalayan river valleys or in the jungles of India and Myanmar or on the frozen slopes of high mountains in China, Peru or East and South Africa continue to subsist. For such tribal groups, eternity of life has just started with artifacts of civilization reaching them through the advances around them. The area particularly beneficial for agricultural advance and so capable of supporting larger population was of river valleys particularly of Egypt, Mesopotamia, riverain plains of India, China and Europe and civilized living developed there. Towns developed on nodal sites and river and coastal anchorages. Trade grew. Indian, Chinese and Baltic regions developed coastal trade. Indian traders were to be seen in Arab lands and in China. The Chinese traders penetrated to all countries and islands in the Pacific or around it. There is recorded evidence of Chinese and Hindu traders visiting Mexico. Hindu teachers and colonizers were welcome in the east as well as in the west of India. Many braved the elements to a welcome in China, Japan, Korea and Vietnam. The Mahayana form of Buddhism that incorporated local deities in the Buddhist pantheon was re-invigorated in the rise of Kanishkan empire in West Asia with the capital city at Peshawer. Soon afterwards it also became part of flourishing Manicheism, a mixture of Zoroastrianism, Hindu-Buddhism and Christ's teachings. The steppes with restricted agriculture and more dependence on sheep raising and horse breeding became overpopulated again and again. They would send abroad peaceful migrants or fighting units to settle in empty lands outside their customary drives. The Aryans that entered Iran or India did not initially believe in rebirth and transmigration of the ever-lasting soul. The Chinese built their formidable western wall to protect overcrowding in their habitat. The Kushan, the Hun and the Mangol invasions of the settled world ensued. The invaders found accommodation in peace or after a struggle but soon they would be fighting, along with those who were living there from earlier times, fresh incursion from fresh hordes. A good example is the Thai invasion and occupation of Assam in East India. In the next century they were the new champions of inhabitants of Assam against the designs of the Delhi Government, first of the Mughals and later of the British. In the meanwhile, the Thais intermixed with the Assamese and like other Hindus started revering the cow. Steam engines and later the internal combustion engine started modern communications only in the nineteenth century. The communications earlier were primitive depending on power of wind or water flow or on horses, oxen and tame elephants. In spite of poor communications, gigantic migrations, armed attacks as well as peaceful diffusion of populace and ideas took place. Ancient Indian and Chinese empires maintained infantry, cavalry and contingents of elephants. Alexander fought his battles by clever positioning of his cavalry and infantry attacks. The empire of Darius and of Egypt crumbled before the Roman Legions who attacked in massed and disciplined infantry formations. Hannibal defended his Libyan empire in Africa and invaded Rome in force taking his elephants there via Spain, France and Switzerland, but later the Roman empire with superior sailing ships was victorious over Charthage and eliminated it from the Mediterranean world. The strength and patriotic zeal of the Romans were responsible for the Roman peace in the then world and provided safety of the Roman roads. Equally large empires of Darius, China and Kanishka were less successful in the globalization sense. The self-assessed success of the British empire almost made it look like a successor to the Roman empire. The British empire however benefited from the newly risen applications of modern science and technology. The communication had improved to a higher order. Their unscrupulous chase of success was a lesson which was later perfected by miscellaneous dictatorships among the world powers, notably Germany, Russia and Japan. The British empire was dissolved after two world wars and totally new device of non-violent non-cooperation movement in their Indian empire after the protest leader, M.K. Gandhi had first tested his ammunition of non-violent protest in South Africa against the apartheid practiced there.

Going back to the world stage before the rise of the Iranian empire of Darius, the pastoral Aryans who fought from chariots spread from their unknown habitat now presumed to be south of the China silk route and soon occupied as the ruling class in both Iran and India and both sections of Aryans regarded themselves as the genuine article. The sacred books of the Aryans, the Vedas, were composed in the Punjab (India). Around that time, the Harrapan civilization was spread from the Punjab, across Rajasthan and Gujarat to Balochistan and across eastern Iran to the Kabul valley. The Harrapans, Aryans and the tribal cultures from South India and Afghanistan combined to form the Hindu culture as christened by the Iranians who regarded the tribes in the north of Iran living on the slopes of the Hindu Kush including the general population of Afghanistan and India as Hindu while reserving the epithet of Arya for themselves. The Aryan bloom however occurred in India. Besides the Vedas and Shastras compiled in India, the Indian Aryas were the first to develop a classical language Sanskrit believed to be the mother language of the human race. They developed its grammar and alphabet. Even in the early days Hinduism spread to Korea and Japan where it is still practised as Shintoism. Hindus had a great thinker, Gautam Buddha, who experimented with various religious and worship themes taught in India like the doctrines of Patanjali and Jainism and developed his own system for salvation of the soul viz aiming at Buddhist nirvana or freedom from repeated births and deaths. Buddhism was just an identification of those who followed the way of Dharma, of right action and the middle path of control of desires without falling into the morass of materialism. Hindus from various parts of India spread with the Indian trade and commerce to all countries of East and West Asia from their major centres in Varanasi and East India or from Taxila and Kashmir. The professors of Hinduism from the Nalanda University spread the peculiar faith of the Tibetan Lamaism in Tibet, a mixture of Buddhism and local magical religion. An ancient civilization that grew almost in isolation in the city states of Greece is considered to be the starter of the European culture hued with Christian faith carried to Europe by the Roman slaves from Greece and Greek colonies of Asia Minor.

Around 3000 B.C. history began in the middle east. King Sargon of Akkad established an empire in Mesopotamia. Babylon stayed as a major centre of culture upto 569 B.C. when it was over-run by the Iranians. The Chaldean king Nebuchadnazar (6th century B.C.) is worth a mention and so is Hammurabi, the first law giver around 2700 B.C. Much is known about this region because of the use of their Cuniform writing on clay tablets by a pointed stylus. The tablets were then sun-dried and stored in the libraries attached to temples or the seats of justice. Piles of such tablets from the ruins of various cities have been deciphered.

The next turning point in history of the world occurred when Columbus discovered America with the firm belief that earth was round like a globe, towards the end of the 15th century A.D. This led to the looting of Mexican and Aztec riches of South America by the Spanish adventurers and the spread of the Roman Catholic form of Christianity there. Thus began the modern age, in mutual jealousy and spirit of adventure of the Europeans.

3

EMPIRES AND NATION STATES

The early empires in India or China were only consolidation of small states into a large state under sovereign emperor or Maharaja. In India, it was considered the duty of a ruler to expand his kingdom for the glory of himself and his subjects. The empires seemed to exist with the agreement of the subjects who had the right to pull down a cruel or inept king. Alongwith kingdoms and empires, India had always a few republics governed by elected rulers. In Bengal, even in the seventh century even an emperor was elected. This elected ruler became the founder of the Pal dynasty which lasted about three centuries. China had the Han empire in the north and a Wei empire in the south.

Nanda dynasty ruled an empire in India from their capital city of Pataliputra (modern Patna) and their rule was followed by the Maurya dynasty of Chanakya fame. Chanakya with Chandragupta, a natural son of the Nanda emperor, gave a fight to the governor of Taxila, a Greek appointee of Alexander the Great after the defeat of Raja Porus of Jhelum. Chandragupta Maurya became the first Maurya emperor at Pataliputra, to whose court the Greek overlord of West Asia, Seleucus, sent an ambassador Megasthenes who has left glowing account of the Mauryan capital and the Indian society. Persian empire was conquered by Alexander, and his empire extended from Greece in the west to Lahore in the east and to the Black Sea in the north and Alexandria in the south. Indian traders opened up most countries on the rim of the Indian Ocean and Indian scholars and saints were very much welcome in South East Asia and in West Asia. A tradition of an Indian trader or banker in most west Asian villages has been there upto the beginning of the nineteenth century.

Indian adventurers, scholars and sailors opened up the South Asian countries for trade with India and middle east. Asian hordes, Sakas, Kushans and Huns marauded all over the known world and were later to become a threat to the Roman empire along with tribal braves of Northern Europe. First 'globalization' of trade and communications was attempted in the Roman empire of antiquity that followed the dissipation of the Greek empire. Roman-led armies assured the freedom of the roads and Roman currency was the medium of exchange in the empire. After the barbarians had uprooted the Roman empire, Europe was salvaged by the spread of Christianity there. In the holy Roman empire, the Pope held the ecclesiastic authority and an emperor at Vienna the temporal authority. The Christian empire broke up into separate nation states under sundry kings. The nation states became real nations after the thirty years war which impoverished and weakened the whole of Europe except England and Holland. The first European empire builders outside Europe were Portugal and Spain after the modern age had begun on the discovery of America. The slogan of might is right prevailed and a gory conquest of the American tribes or rather their elimination from any rights in their land ensued. The Spanish conquest of South America is held as most cruel occupation of foreign land. The Spanish religious authorities withheld cruel treatment of natives only when they accepted Christianity of the masters. The advanced native culture and their holy practices were forbidden. The Mayan people of Yucatan were subdued as late as 1546. Only now after the recent sweeping wave of democracy in the world, have the South Americans awakened to their ancient customs. Mexico, Cuba, Argentina feel now more liberated than before.

The world became a medley of nations after the great war. The weaker nations could remain free only under the jealous watch of USA and Russia.

The establishment of the UN by the victorious allies after the World War ushered a new dimension to the international scene. The advances of science and technology and the wave of democracy sweeping over the world under the umbrella of the UN, especially after the bowing out of arms competition by Russia when confronted by the American resolve to be at the top of the armament dung-heap. The world has become comparatively free from aggressive expansion of stronger countries. The diplomacy of non-alignment adopted by most anti-imperialist countries also assisted in better understanding between major powers. This has become a welcome period for setting world affairs in the direction of peace and friendship than allow a drift to another war and possible suicide of civilization. Already the governance of many world affairs is carried out internationally with the consent of the nations of the world. The diplomatic skill now consists of cooperating with each other and the UN activated multinational commissions. The nations with a strong UN can escape the tragedy of the frogs under king stork and be able to impress democratic decision making to any strong power that might try to bully them.

In the sixteenth century, it was the turn of the imperialist countries of Europe to globalize trade and attempt to civilize the world on the new found strength from applying new developments in science and technology to the winning of wars along with their complete lack of ethical scruples in dealing with others with an assumed assurance of superiority in culture and belief. The British globalization of trade helped them win an empire in India and they succeeded in securing their world wide trade by establishing colonies and outposts in every part of the world. Indians were the junior partners in British aggrandizement particularly in China and Africa. Where the Indian rulers had never fought any wars of aggression outside India, the British Indian Army fought in every continent to preserve the British empire except in America, and the American colonies were the first to slip out of British control. With the demise of the British empire, other European countries also soon lost their empires. After two world wars, the scene was of a crowd of nation states, who are now attempting to come together to save the weaker nations and all people from the tyranny of wars and the common man from the negation of human rights. The feudal order and the rule of princes and kings is practically gone now and every nation state has an incentive to be counted as a democracy with a stake in the success of the United Nations to which they all belong. Thus they may not fall prey after isolation to a single or one of many super powers. Post-modern period of the world started with the defeat of imperialism and signing of a United Nations charter.

We have not mentioned the contribution of the Muslim Caliphate first established at Baghdad and later at Constantinople. The Muslims believed in the divine right of Muslim authority to extend over all lands held by non-believers and in their hey-day they controlled whole of India, Middle East, the slave trade, and the trade routes between the Middle East and India and further east. The Muslim forces had success also in the south and west of Europe but the Muslim power was reduced to a pacified Turkey after the great war, or after the earlier rout of the Caliph's forces at Vienna and expulsion of Muslim control from Spain. The remains of Muslim conquest are to be seen as architectural wonders in Spain, Egypt, North Africa, Turkey and India. There was a short-lived Japanese empire and empires of the axis powers like Germany and Italy. These were swept away in the world wars. A new Communist empire, a successor to Czarist empire, through socialist revolution and expansion, was formed in Europe which collapsed after the end of the cold war and enlightened policies of Gorbachov of the Soviet Union.

Parallel to the growth of European empires, the world religions tightened their hold on their flocks. All religions tried to have more converts excepting Hinduism since Hindus regard all human beings as being Hindu, only, some people do not know this. A fresh claim was made by Swami Vivekananda's speeches at the World Congress of Religions held in Chicago in 1895. It became clear that conversion from native religion tended to denationalize the converts which only suited the imperial rulers. New-Confucianism at peace with the prayers and right living of the Buddhists unified China. Shankaracharya's exposition of the Gita and growing Bhakti (a doctrine of devotion and love) or love of God and the Muslim Sufism unified most of India. The reformation, industrial revolution in Europe and the example of Spain and Portugal getting rich from their hold in newly discovered America set all the European countries on the path of lucrative trade and colonialist exploitation of the east and the west. They also assumed moral authority over the non-Christians. Inside Europe, Sweden was thwarted by France and Russia, Germany by England, and Russia was thwarted by Japan in Asia. The game of threats and alliances ended only in the rise of communist power and the two world wars. The Soviet Union burnt its fingers in Afghanistan and liquidated itself when faced with competition in arms build up during the cold war with USA. Imperialism breathed its last after the British lost control of India and met democratic opposition of the world for their attempt with France to pry out the Suez Canal from the control of Egypt. The US President was not satisfied with the quiet status of sole super power of the world; he proclaimed that they intended to crush all opposition to their super-power status. The Americans took spirited action against the Muslim powers who they thought were behind the upsurge of Islamic reaction against the hegemony of USA and Israel in the middle east.

The time seems to be past for any nation to try to enlarge its space. Even the trusteeship districts of the world are likely to achieve their desired freedom under the rejuvenated UN of the near future. The nations have to think in terms of increasing their wealth in the training and achievements of their citizens within the country or in the international sphere. They have to exert in specializations like science and technology, medicine or management and cooperate with other countries and the UN agencies for the conquest of space and the enrichment of the biosphere. Every nation is invited to advancement of culture, peace and friendship.

The world is now witnessing the US-led globalization of trade and commerce. There is intense pressure for restructuring the UN and its Security Council. A new kind of global nationalism is in the offing that will desire democratic structure of UN and equip it with an international law and international backing to look after the internal and external peace of all nations. An expanded Security Council will be formed and the veto could be replaced by a supreme peace council of chosen elders of the world which will be the veto wielding authority and final court of appeal. For global peace and global prosperity, peaceful coexistence and assurance of equal human rights for all will have to be forthcoming. For inspiration, one could look at the Hindu-Buddhist world of international co-operation and peace (300 B.C. to 200 A.D.) extending from Japan to Volga and from Turkestan to Sri Lanka, a frontier-less region of exchange of knowledge and goods.

4

SOME UNFORGETABLES

Every culture and every country had its leaders, but the names of only a few have filtered down to this day. Some are only leaders of conquering armies or of valient defence. To name a few: Thutmos of Egypt and Nebuchadnazar of Babylon, Julius Caeser, Fredrick the Great, Gustavus Adolphus of Sweden, Chauhan and Ghori, Napoleon, Churchil and many others. A recent exceptional leader also merits mention here is Ho Chi Minh of Vietnam who freed his country after the world war from so many hunters: France, USA, China and Japan.

Thutmos is included in above list as he defeated the Syrians and their allies in 1500 B.C. and subdued the entire Mediterranean belt which Napoleon could not do in the nineteenth century. The arts and wealth of ancient Egypt was phenomenal at that time. The temples of Thebes, his capital city were filled with golden statues of Egyptian deities. The Egyptian wealth rested on devoted labour of the superstitious peasants befuddled with convincing stories of resurrection of buried mummies and the everlasting life of the faithful. The god Mardul's favourite Nebuchdnazar of Babylon annihilated Egypt's power few centuries before Christ and controlled the trade route with the East. He was the builder of the hanging gardens of Babylon. The Huns invasion of Asia and Europe was started by Attila and continued by his deputy Mehergul. The Huns when intruded into India were speedily assimilated and became defenders from other tribal attacks. In Europe their excursions lasted a century.

The Huns are depicted in history as the most cruel foreign invaders of Europe with scant regard for man or god. The Turkish tribes in their new found Islamic enthusiasm for *jehad* behaved no less cruelly when they over-ran Afghanistan and Punjab having Hindu-Buddhist rulers. The same can be said about Kublai Khan, the usurper Mongol emperor of China at Canton or the Japanese in their one-sided warfare in Korea and China in the last century. The Mongols were absorbed in China as Chinese citizens. Repeatedly, the Mongol horsemen devastated Arab and Iranian lands in Asia. The rape of the Arab empire of the Caliphs by Changez Khan and its destruction later by his son Halaku in 1238 A.D. is heart wrenching.

The world is more indebted to antiquity for the discoveries and inventions they made in learning, music, architecture, medicine or the art of living. They emphasized virtue and healthy life. They were in favour of humanism and co-operative living. Great men of antiquity were the philosophers, prophets, poets and mystics and those who ached for human happiness. The list starts with those who banished slavery from whole of India in about 2000 B.C. The ancient Hindus believed that each individual had a special talent or aptitude for specific calling. In the absence of real tests for aptitudes and fully believing in rebirth according to one's deeds of past lives, they placed each infant in the profession or caste of his father. This system was not of much harm since the education and professional training was available to a child first and foremost in the family usually from the father. Upto recent times, the caste remained the anchor of Indian civilization. The subsistence level agriculture, professions and trade continued enriching only the tax collectors or the builders of temples.

The Hindus took to democracy like duck to water. They had in the past experienced both democracy and kingship. The succession in kingship always resulted in civil wars and discomfort to the public. Democratic election of rulers seemed to offer less hardship. The village panchayats or village self-rule had lasted throughout the centuries. The non-violent struggle was perfected by Mahatma Gandhi after successful confrontation with apartheid in South Africa. He used such a struggle to win Indian independence in 1947. The world will remain healthy if it accepts non-violence for reforms, pluralism, co-existence and passion for human rights for all. To reach this stage, the contributions of the leaders of the French Revolution, Communists who took over Czarist Russia, Garibaldi of Italy, D'Valera of Ireland and Lumumba of Congo, Martin Luther King, Jr. of USA and many others have to be remembered. The future lies with self-less service and recognition of coexistence of all people.

Among the leaders of antiquity, there are unknown ordinary men and women who experimented with nature's bounty in plants and animals, formulated many cures for various ailments, many recipes for the kitchen, designed temples and tombs, invented games and pastimes and were fore-runners of Kalidas, Shakespeare and Schiller, Tolstoy or Premchand. Many an ancient philosopher, law giver or mystic was raised to the pedestal of a God by the grateful public. Krishna, the hero of the Mahabharata who expounded the Gita, was accepted as God incarnate in temples all over India. The inventor of the wheel, the ancient agro-scientist who produced the Basmati Rice or discovered the healing powers of the Neem tree are forgotten.

Leaders of the recent past who have established the high road to advances in science and technology and the supremacy of observation, reason and logic, led the revolution in farms and industry and the use of computers for higher production and better control of environment. We have to ponder over the situation in the absence of George Fox, Abraham Lincoln, Faraday, Darwin, Einstein, Neuman or Tagore.

For the future progress of mankind, a different set of leaders are now important. These are the path-finders who have shaped modern science and technology. They have pulled out the world from tall claims of rituals, magic and blind faith or lack of trust in logic and human reason or in factual observations and planned experiments. Such a list begins with Newton and now remembered names of ancient Indian astronomers and mathematicians reaching to the inimitable Einstein. Besides the leaders of science who are no more, we have a whole lot of them working and theorizing all over the world. Listing such stalwarts from Vyas to Bernard Shaw, Tansen and Mozart to Ravi Shankar, George Fox to Mahatma Gandhi, Ashoka to Mandela, etc here would be not possible. In every field, world wisdom and culture, arts and sciences have been enriched by the genius of individual men and women of many nations and many countries.

The imposing structure of science and technology, mathematics, electronics and biochemistry has been built in the last three centuries. Sky is the limit for the ever rising human achievements in the coming centuries and millennia so long as we continue a purposeful existence without compromising it by needless strife and quarrels. Already democratic and willing cooperation have established many departments of world governance. Many international agreements from intergovernmental conferences under the aegis of the UN, supported by experts from many countries pave the way for progress without hurdles. The successes already achieved gives us hope that the humanistic policies of development will soon banish abject poverty from the world and the trend of equality and freedom will become universal reality. There will now be a new flowering of civilization giving avenues of actualization to all persons of ability. One can visualize application and advance in many subjects like cybernetics, treatment of burns and wounds, doubling of expected average human life world-wide, multi-dimensional geometry, total (system) analysis, robotics, increased mental abilities, computer controlled machines and new results in humanist economics and human centered evolution.

5

ESSENTIALS FOR LIFE

For life to exist, the essentials of living space, breathable air, potable water, food and a minimum count for human contact and simulation are necessary. Migration of tribes and communities or individuals has occurred because of the felt scarcity of even one of these essentials. The repeated ice ages drove everything before the advancing ice. Remains of forests and animals are now visible in the north of Asia and America from these times. In the dim past, early migration of African bipeds occurred from Africa to Asia. There is evidence that the earth tilted materially about two billion years ago, that will bring large area of sunshine into the gloom of northern latitudes. Some anomalous discoveries of crude might be the result of the tilting of the earth about two billion years ago.

(a) LAND

Desertification also drives life away as must have happened in the early history of the riverain region where the legendary Saraswati flowed in east Rajasthan. The scattered population of deserts is still on the move. The land communications hardly exist for the dwellers of dense forests and the subsistence level existence is their lot. Similar is the condition of people in dense forests of Nicobars, Australia or cold heights of Tibet or the Andes. It is the pressure of population that drove the people of the British Isles to Australia and New Zealand. The pressure of population and the lure of opportunity drove armed hordes of

Asian steppes to lord over the rest of Asia and Europe. The lure of opportunity has egged on many daring spirits to migrate abroad from Europe, India or China. The Celts strode across Northern Europe with zeal for combat and glory. Trade and commerce has been the leading star for many migrants, particularly Chinese, Arabs, Indians and Englishmen. The Japanese and the Scandinavians have hunted fish all over the seas. Newly acquired oil wealth has made the Arab countries the Eldorado for many struggling youths of other lands. The current globalization is creating new centres of attraction. In the near past, the British attention to nodal points in maritime trade made Hong Kong, Singapore, Aden and Cape Town and many other ports attract many migrants to make them flourishing centres. Commerce by air has created new oasis of wealth like Dubai. Casinos have bloated Las Vegas, the Riviera in Southern France and Kathmandu in Nepal. Internal unrest has resulted in migration out of Kashmir, Nepal and Tibet and the minorities are still spilling out of Bangladesh. Security of life and one's possessions is the first concern of people after the essentials enumerated above.

The recent Tsunami wave destroyed many coastal communities and their fishing gear in India and other neighbouring lands. The Japanese have struggled for long with natural catastrophies like earthquakes and sea wave havoc. Cyclonic storms have affected the usefulness of some coastal areas in Andhra or in Florida. Even the exact cause of enormously high sea wave in the aftermath of cyclones is not yet understood. The most probable explanation is the truncation of the deeper sea water whirl that follows the atmospheric cyclone over the sea. The land is made fertile by river floods, no doubt, but river floods every year devour the habitability of the land as has been the experience of cities and villages along the Brahamaputra or the Mississipi before the latter was tamed. China has suffered in the past from uncontrolled floods in rivers. Cutting down of the shore by action of sea waves can now be avoided by appropriate off shore structures. People need some spot of land/or a floating platform to set up their house. Men are adapted to life in coastal areas based on fishing or coastal trade. Primitive craft took emigrants across rivers and oceans. Sails on ships were used for speed. The countries around the Baltic Sea and around the Mediterranean Sea were often raiding each other using men-of war converted from sailing boats. For extra speed, they had rows of slaves plying oars to assist the helmsman proceed forward at will and to allow the fighting men in the upper deck to fight it out with the enemy equipped in the same way. Roman victory over Cleopatra of Egypt is familiar from the movies on the theme. Ancient warlike campaigns were mainly across land as already recounted. Wars were always a major threat to peaceful evolution of civilization. The hope of peace now lies in the success of the United Nations. But the short cut diplomacy of wars is taking time to die out. In reality, the fight should not be to expand possession of land by displacing other occupants; the need is to fight adverse elements and stop desertification or to develop areas covered by dense forests or swamps. Canadians have created underground habitations in the frozen north. People are spending their lives on floating junks near coasts of China or India.

For growing food also, people need land. Agricultural advances now make it possible to have special plantations in saline soils or in backwaters. There is growing research in developing fish farms in coastal zones both in the sea as well as on land by transplanting tiny fish to artificial fish ponds created on land, and for better use of marine parks under development. Industrial management of natural or man-made forests will augment forest resources. Mushroom and lotus cultivation saves land. Planners have to be watchful for preserving the soil quality. The estimated increase of waste land in the wheat belt in India has been alarming. The agricultural extension services have to particularly concern themselves to the planting of soil enriching crops periodically. Acidification of soils can also be mended.

(b) WATER

Due to sharp rise in population and increased amount of water being used in industry, sanitation and air cooling etc, water shortage is staring most countries in the face. If saline water is available, it can be used after treatment with chemicals or by distillation. Large amount of energy is required. This is proposed to be ensured by nuclear generation of power. The accent now in most countries is on harvesting rain water by ensuring that it does not flow to waste and is stored either on surface tanks or by charging into earth at suitable depth. India has a gigantic flood control and rainwater use scheme up her sleeve. It might be carried out in the next couple of decades. A beginning has already been made. The excess rain water or water from the stream carrying water past a village or city can be stored in tanks specially built in the city or near the village. Deep bores can give potable water, while sub-soil water is easy to get but can be used for human consumption only after treatment. Quality of drinking water is now laid down in detail regarding dissolved elements and compounds and the specifications should be met. On account of water shortage, water for farming and miscellaneous purposes is now widely reclaimed from city sewage purification ventures recommended almost for every city in the world. Water treatment plants must avoid release of harmful chemicals. The national water resources are vulnerable to over exploitation and contamination. Careful protection measures have to be worked out. Some cities have dual water supply system for economy in expenditure. Flood control gives large quantity of water as well as protects cities on the banks from flood damage. Cities of Bihar state in India and in the Brahmaputra valley still suffer from floods, while increasing flood control is being attempted. The linking of rivers through canals and artificial or natural lakes is in the plan in India. Fifty years ago one could not imagine that water will become a commercial commodity in India. Now a bottle of drinking water in Delhi costs more than a cup of milk. Conservation of water is now a great slogan throughout the world. Public is bound to take action.

The employment of satellite photography, a tool of modern technology, can monitor the health of crops and forests for the planners. Modern science can also pursue the insect swarms, predict their course and install timely measures for their destruction. It is better to destroy the pests in their natal grounds. Such progress requires the early establishment of a world authority. This exists yet in embryo with recommendatory capability. Food production level can be maintained on less land by use of hydroponics. Enormous amount of water is locked in oceans but is highly saline. Sea water distillation is carried out when coupled with some cheap source of electricity like a nuclear reactor or tidal energy plant. A sustainable ice cover in high altitude glaciers and polar ice caps is an assurance of water supply for ever, provided there is no upheaval in nature. The suspected slow heating of the earth has set scientists to investigate the causes and eliminate the release from human activity on earth of harmful gases into the atmosphere. A recommendation exists to use better gases for the cooling cycle in refrigeration and air-conditioning. Sea water connects people and provides cheaper transportation of goods and of crude in container ships and tankers. Research has shown a fast as well as cheaper mode of towing submerged platforms laden with goods. Such towed submerged boat trains will soon become common in a future peaceful united world. Submerged tanker trains can very likely compete with pipelines on land or dangling from floating buoys in the sea. This might become common practice in another couple of centuries.

(c) FOOD

Food is necessary for human existence. Food that is seasonally popular is also a part of offering to deities as part of religious practice so dear to most people. Only the lotus eaters could get all the food they want from nature without any labour. For growing all other food crops, one has to put in timely labour and procure seeds, manure and insecticides and take steps to protect the ripe crop from birds etc. At first, people lived isolated and depended on gathering forest produce and hunting some game. Later with the invention of agriculture or on possessing herds of tame animals, men would settle down in villages and take advantage of numbers for co-operative farm labour in place of commune type farming earlier. The luxury of private possession was achieved and men were keen to amass wealth for their children. The rudiments of capitalism and private family life started very early. After thousands of years, copper and bronze tools were available and we speak of copper age and bronze age. Later, iron was also used by ancient civilizations. The iron pillar constructed some time before Christ can still be seen standing in the open for thousands of years near Delhi. Bullock power and iron studded plough-shares increased food production. Indian farmers, who had made a success of subsistence farming for centuries, are now in great demand where in some countries, new land is to be ploughed for growing more food. If the size of the farm is large, machine farming on commercial scale is recommended. India has large farms for production of rice and wheat, or for cash crops like tea, coffee, cocoa or cotton and mulberry trees (for silk production). Some other plantations are being begun particularly for paper production, for fuel and for diesel substitute oil extraction. Production and export of sugar was a success story of Bengal. Crops of oil seeds are grown almost in all agricultural lands. Indian tea, Chinese silk and Egyptian cotton are world famous. USA and Canada have shown phenomenan yields of wheat. Green revolution in the Punjab brought bumper crops of wheat using new varieties of seeds developed in Mexico and in India under the inspiring leadership of Dr. M.S. Swaminathan. India is producing 65 million tons of wheat compared to the figure of 6.5 million tons in 1947 or before independence and 200 million tons of other foodgrains compared to 12 million tons in 1947. The storage of grains and agricultural produce including cold storage as well as in mud coated straw sylos in the open and protective measures against pilferage by rodents have increased the availability of food in countries like India which are now exporting wheat and rice.

Rice in abundance is the staple food of Asia. Increased production results from larger farm size and co-operative use of high capacity machines which is routinely done now in the Punjab. Similar measures will help Africa in getting rid of periodical famines. With purposeful effort and help from the international community, world should become free from the threat of famine within this century. For adequate nourishment of children, large scale production of milk is necessary. India has considerable experience in this field which can be availed of by other countries. Already most Indian states have milk schemes in which the milk producing households in villages are provided cows from excellent stock and the milk is collected and distributed by cooperatives or large firms. Food shortage in some countries is often because of extreme poverty and lack of purchasing power for the food that in available. The access to sustenance has to be kept outside the calculation of normal trade and profit. The right to be assured of adequate food is a basic requirement. The grain exporting countries will reserve large stock of grain and by periodic replacement of the stocked grain keep it fresh and usable as reserves to be drawn in case of emergencies and famine situations. The FAO would keep track of withdrawals from such stocks and their inspection periodically. This should be possible within this century. It is surmised that 150 million children are under weight. Nourishment has to be assured to all of them in the world acting as one family. Hybrid plants are vigorous. Sterile rice and a dwarfing gene have been identified in Japan and in China. It is expected that there will soon be large production gain for rice. For such research, access to a large range of genetic material is necessary besides an integrated supply of nutrients. There could be more strategy for eco-technology and evergreen revolution. The agricultural extension is recommending cereal-legume rotation, earth-worm culture, rain-water harvesting and conservation measures e.g. by drip irrigation. There is rural pressure for agro-processing industries. This can be accomplished in the next couple of centuries. A phase of developing rural townships will remove the limitless expansion of slums in big towns. Large scale urbanization is now occurring also in developing countries. This will mean perforce conversion to machine farming in large farms. The number of persons engaged in agriculture is now one-tenth of what it was in 1930 for feeding the world. It is projected that now it can be reduced to only one million people for feeding the whole world with four-fold increase of population from 1930. Agricultural output and a stable population will come in balance in next few centuries of vigorous action.

Fish make an important food item in the whole world. The supply of ocean fish is not infinite and measures are adopted to guard fisheries which are considered under proprietary right of certain nations. Iceland, Japan and Maldives have impressive fishing fleets. Australia is coming up as a leading fish exporter. Poultry and quail have added to the breakfast table and new industry of poultry and quail farming is growing in certain areas. In India, Bihar is making headway in quail farming. Poona has the largest hatchery of poultry in Asia. Scientists have concluded that for an agricultural area to be put to pasture and sheep raising is less bountiful to inhabitants than when it is put to agricultural use. But certain lands can best be useful for sheep raising because of lack of soil quality or of sufficient water. Intensive sale promotion has brought about strong tea drinking habit among Indians. Similar effort is needed to popularize fish in daily food of Indians who are not meat eaters. The silver lining is that a religious text of Bengal makes fish eating without blemish for high caste Hindus. We are in favour of popularizing fish as food in India since the Indian share of marine catch is much less than warranted by its long sea coast and its adventurous fishermen. This will require employing more than one fish factory ship so that the catch is processed on board before returning to port all too frequently. Such a vessel will require large refrigeration plant on board. India has priority right over marine produce within 320 km of its long coastline. Relatively large fluctuation of the sea bottom depth finding sonar echo can easily guide to a promising large marine fishing area in the sea. This experimental deduction can be carried within a minute while the fishing vessel is on its course. The usual echo sounder can easily be modified and data can be processed by a simple computer within minutes. India has already expanded river catches manifold but large amount of tuna catches are possible but not carried out because of lack of resources. Maldives, Japan and Australia are major fishing nations in the Indian Ocean. India is the largest exporter of prawns. Prawn farming is extensively carried out on the west coast. Coconut farming is extensive in the coastal belt of India. Coconut is practically a national fruit after the mango. Fisheries education is well established in many countries including India. At the international level, coordination is carried out by the FAO. Nine regional fisheries bodies have been set up by the FAO. Anchored surface floating rafts provide observations, especially of aggregating tuna. India is producing more than four million tons of fish annually and more catches are expected with the projected exploitation of the deep sea fisheries. Satellite imagery can provide big aid for pin-pointing surface shoaling of skipjack, yellow fish and albacore. Proper regulation of sub-surface long line fishing has to be installed. It is recommended to expand production by all countries of fish meal and fish oil. There is considerable lack of knowledge about bottom trawling grounds and of pelagic fisheries other than sardine and mackerel. Induced breeding and rearing technology has already been mastered for many shell fish, milk fish and mullets. There is considerable scope for the integrated development of fisheries with the utilization of coastal land for suitable plantation crops and livestock. The open sea mariculture has a future in some countries.

With continuous increase in population, the food production has to keep pace. Education and higher standard of life tend to reduce population as observed in northern Europe. (In Taiwan, the number of graduating girls was doubled during 1966 to 1972, and the birth rate was reduced to half). The population is, at current rate of growth, doubling every thirty years. The population has to be stabilized. Some incentives to curtail births have to be kept in force. Much will depend on mutual adjustments to celibacy and adopting of "Brahmacharya" discipline in life, in preference to material birth control measures. This should be possible in this millennium particularly because there will be more education and freedom for women. In advanced European countries of the north, already birth rate has dropped to low figures and they are even out to have some controlled immigration. Human activities influence environment. The international governance will have the authority to keep up global ecological sustainability through training and model environmental laws offered to state governments. The world can accomplish this in the coming millennium.

A threat to the devastation of land is from a fresh ice-age. Without any prior indication ice-caps and glaciers start flowing as ice and destroying everything the following ice encounters. It is surmised that due to change in the ocean circulation because of may-be certain obstacles happening in the straits connecting the oceans, warm waters do not reach the polar regions and ice melts and breaks to flow along the sloping land. It is in the cards that if the straits are kept dredged and widened where necessary, the circulation will not be affected and a new ice age may not occur.

6

HEALTH, MEDICINE AND LONGEVITY

For an active and creative life, good health is of the highest importance. Longevity is also a corollary of good health. It is usually believed that in olden times, those that survived childhood diseases, lived a longer life compared to now. Life was of wholesome application and the pollution in air or water was insignificant. The women throughout the ages had a life of hard work. The responsibility for cooking, cleaning, fetching water and rearing children including checking on their school education were always their functions. They also carried out spinning, weaving and ginning cotton and many other household and cottage industry chores. Men worked in the field or in animal husbandry. They also learnt some craft usually by assisting the family in some way or the other. They preferred simplicity, and love of God and of man. The medical lore was passed on from parents to children. The empirical knowledge about the human body and its ailments and customary cures was common. All kinds of surgery was performed by trained barbers. Brahmans taught medicine but usually its practice was below their dignity. Hakims followed the Greek system of medicine which was not much different from the Indian system. There was great deal of knowledge about herbal remedies. There was no concept of community hygiene except the creation of sanitation workers condemned to this work by birth. Inside the houses, there was cleanliness but public sanitation was missing and people used the jungle and the pond for ablutions. Children suffered most from skin rashes and boils, malaria was rampant. Quinine was discovered much later, but an effective 'glo' creeper served as a preventive remedy. Its water extract was to be taken daily in a small quantity. The average span of life of human beings was rather low. Those who survived childhood lived to about sixty-five. The biblical dream of ninety years was rarely achieved, but the Indian prayers for long life hinted that the Indians regarded hundred years as the allotted old age for men and women. For many diseases, prayers at special shrines sacred to minor divinities looking after the children or controlling epidemics were resorted to. People believed in the efficacy of prayer and incantations by the sick person or recited on his/her behalf by the priests, (a precursor of modern psychotherapy).

Living body is prone to disease and most animals have an instinct for self-treatment. We know from ancient bones from burial places that bone tremors have been the curse for many ancient lives. The armies on the march had the service of a field hospital as unearthed in Europe from the days of Roman occupation in the second century A.D. Ruins of Pompei have disclosed a nursing home in the house of a physician. Record exists of the first hospital at Paris Medical School. Roger Bacon (1214-1294) carried out some experimental research. In the middle ages, Caliphate Medical College flourished at Cordova. Jewish, Egyptian, Chinese and the Hindu medical knowledge was significant. Mummification showed intimate knowledge of human anatomy. The oldest pharmacopeia has been unearthed in the Eban papyrus discovered in an Egyptian pyramid. The Atharva Veda mentions many cures and curing incantations. The Arabs compiled the ancient medical wisdom and transmitted it to Europe.

Europe was shaken by the great epidemic in 1345 A.D., and as a result about half of its population died. Last great epidemic occurred in Marseilles in 1720 A.D.

Quarantine measures were first taken in Italy against the spread of infectious disease. Only in the twentieth century, man could understand, through modern medicine, the spreading of the infectious diseases and could take preventive measures and hunt for cures. Diseases like small pox, leprosy and polio have been practically wiped out. New diseases like the heart disease and AIDS have spread, but these are not infectious. The Hindus had comparatively lower count of sexually concerned diseases. They have religious inducement for Brahmacharya or sexual abstinence before marriage and they mostly believed in monogamy. Indiscriminate sex is held responsible for AIDS and Indians now also report spread of this disease. Indiscriminate sex is evidently growing in spite of doctrinaire morality and because of increased personal liberty from family pressures and social controls.

Indian system of healthcare relies on daily Yoga (a system of physical exercises without any AIDS through simple body postures), and breath control. It is claimed that breathing in a systematic way can cure many diseases. They claim to control arthritis as well as heart disease, obesity, etc. Herbal massages are quite popular and India is the destination of many health tourists from abroad. The health lore, widely learnt now is:

(i) Daily care of teeth. The instruction is to rinse the mouth with plain water after eating any food.

(ii) Daily exercise for about 15 minutes including yogic exercises with or without the morning walk.

(iii) Over-tiring oneself is to cease. Think well before committing yes or no.

(iv) No use worrying since worry solves no problems, analyse the situation and take prompt action.

(v) For desirable good opinion of others about yourself, you must regard them worthy too.

(vi) Have high ambition and constantly take action for its realization.

I have found that some information about very common homeopathic medicines for some complaints is very useful as first aid, but as early as possible a competent physician should be consulted. All foods have some special disease prevention property which can easily be learnt including the foods that should be avoided. In India, medical science is known as Ayurveda or science of long life. The ancients aimed at a life of hundred years: first twenty-five years to be spent on formal education and training. With advances in knowledge and specialization in hundreds of fields, the span of hundred years of life is too small. George Bernard Shaw has argued that immediate aim should be raised to a life of one hundred and fifty years. Then the formal learning years can be somewhat extended with a refresher period of learning upto two years when one has crossed midway that is at seventy-five years of age.

Among ancient doctors, most prominent is Hippocrates of the Hippocratic oath fame. Dhanvantri, the great Indian physician, is almost regarded as a god. Other important names are Harvey (he clarified the circulation of blood in the body), Varalius of Brussells (physiology), Sanctorius of Padua who invented the clinical thermometer, Pasteur (understanding of infectious diseases), Lister, and Flavius. Anaesthesia was developed in American hospitals. A French army doctor identified the malaria causing mosquito. Messmer (1733-1815) initiated treatment of psycho-somatic complaints. Science of bacteriology, very useful for medicine was developed in the last couple of centuries. Surgical circumcision was started in Egypt in 2300 B.C. First text book on Gynaecology was used in Mesopotamia in 2000 B.C. Indian medicine was widely disseminated by Indian Hindu-Buddhist scholars throughout the known world in the heyday (300 B.C. to 700 A.D.) of Hindu expansion in Asia. Hygienic preparation of food was a fetish with the Hindus. They even advocated that the cook must be of a truthful and loving nature. Sewage pharmacology was a subject of Hindu medicine. Now a new pharmacology is developing based on marine plants and animals.

Modern medicine has made tremendous advances. Many new technologies like X-ray photography, sono-graphy, ultra-sound scan of brain tumors, use of electron microscopy, nuclear magnetic resonance, radioactivity, gamma rays, nuclear medicine, oxygen for easy breathing in special situations etc. etc. Blood characterization and transfusion have been yoked to modern diagnosis or modern treatments. Laser has reduced complicated treatment of incipient blindness to an OPD concern with no hospitalization. The invention of spectacles has helped millions live a normal life inspite of defective vision. Plastic surgery has been carried out in Hindu medicine, but it is now a common treatment. Cure of burn injuries is advancing as a separate expertise. In fact, the number of branches of medicine and their specialization is mind boggling. Medical education like most education is now requiring life-long application. Modern practice is to run short courses for few specialists all over the world so that new knowledge is made available to the common man and the common medical practitioner. One likes to believe now that the purpose if any of the existence of this world is the continuation of life so long as the human biosphere lasts. From every side, the belief is strengthened that, but for an overwhelming calamity, the human intellect will steer successfully the evolution of human beings for the practical eternity. Population will be stabilized relatively soon. At one time, it was in fashion to be ascetic and stay away from sexual reproduction. Birth control by contraceptives is now encouraged. More education and better standard of life shrinks population also. The option of ascetic life is likely to become again fashionable. One is surprised at many reputed foreign scholars queuing up at the meditation centres in India. Mother Teresa found her life fulfilment as a Christian in India.

Medical research and medical knowledge are increasing very fast. The medical treatment has become very expensive. Some patients or their close kin pray for early death and escape from the mounting hospitals bills. The general practitioner of medicine should be well grounded in all basic systems of medicine or integrated medicine and be in a position to advise about the most efficient treatment for the complaint. Modern diagnosis should be quite inexpensive and available to the private practitioner. A five star hotel like hospital indoor facility may not be indicated for any disease but for the seriously ill. Male or female nursing attention should be available at homes at reasonable prices since love and care at home can work miracles. Insurance companies and NGO's can take a lead in this. The community welfare bodies could have in employment some qualified medical volunteers or professionals who can be required to visit the old and the disabled at their residence at a low fee. Such organized universal medical attention would be built into the new urbanization as well as in the rural health centres. The scheme is expected to work like clockwork in the next few centuries in the peacefully developing world. Future will also introduce gene therapy. Already, some people are starting preserving some stem cells from the birth of the baby for any eventual necessity. Transplanting of organs would become common place along with compatible material transplants. There has been considerable advance in the supply and fitting of artificial limbs. The education and training of people will rid them of blind trust in horoscopes, astrology and use of magical incantations and sacrifices in favour of a deity of one sort or the other. The individual's personal data of blood type or particular preventive medicine recommended for regular use would be stored in computer for reference by medical attendant in the community. Everyone in the interest of oneself and one's well-wishers will periodically update his or her personal data fil by including also frankly, his ambitions, his own estimate of his qualities of valour, cowardice, nature (suspicious or trusting), disposition (charitable or miserly) or a short pen picture of himself/herself. Such data can be of use to society with the permission of the individual or for analysis of his life's work after he ceases to live.

•

7

TOOLS AND TECHNOLOGY

Animals have instincts that assist in self-preservation. Man has the distinctive characteristic of creative intelligence with which to preserve his gene. Man creates tools and uses them for his purpose. Technology is the art and craft which helps him prepare his tools and put them to various uses and to improve them. Materials technology is concerned with the preparation and understanding of materials. Use of better materials more appropriate for a particular tool or its purpose is basic in the preparation of the tool. When man just emerged from animal category by walking on two feet using two limbs as hands, the only readily available materials surrounding him were forest twigs, sand, dirt and stones. In the initial period known as the stone age, he fashioned digging and fighting tools of stone. Later, he progressed to copper age, bronze age and iron age. Now he has reached the age of semi-conductors and is knocking at the entrance of the age of bio-molecules. The knowledge of all previous ages is readily available to him. He has just about graduated from the hard school of violence and "might is right". Very early in his story he proved his skill and superiority in dealing with other species. One to one, he is weaker than hundreds of species but by clever ingenuity and use of tools he runs zoos and aquariums for exhibiting to his children. The biggest challenge came to him from other members of his own species: other tribes, foreign nations and ambitious imperialists and dictators or empire builders. The up-scaling of weapons has brought about the invention of weapons of mass destruction as demonstrated in the U.S. bombing of two cities in Japan. Chemical gases were invented and used in the first World War, but the combatants practically stayed away from their use in the second World War, though the allegations of chemical and bacteriological warfare were bandied about. There was sudden awareness that war must be outlawed. Faltering steps in that direction have been taken by forming United Nations. The seeds of failure are already there in the provision of veto with the five victorious countries of the second World War. Though the experience of the veto is not so negative since sometimes the oppressive elements have engineered majority for themselves and the only resort left for justice is through the veto of a clear thinking veto wielding power. But for the democratic decision to prevail in future the veto should be abolished or exercised by the general assembly on the recommendation of four or five respected seniors diplomats chosen as a permanent Sanity or Peace Council beforehand by the General assembly periodically.

In the past, the science and technology have been prostituted by the security needs of each nation. Now when war is outlawed practically, the tools and technology will be put to their primary use for civilized life and continuation of the human gene. Civilized life has thousands of needs. For dwellings, cottages and palaces were built. For recreation, swimming pools, country clubs, theatres, and amusement parks were built. Adventure sports, mountain climbing and ski-jumps were recognized. Tourism industry is flourishing based on wonders to see, and hotel resorts to facilitate this. Colleges, courts and libraries have been built. The wonder instruments have been radio, television, personal computers, tape recorded music systems, holography (three dimensional image) etc. We are now having rapid progress in electronics and are on the threshold of using DNA molecules for superior control and intelligence apparatus. High technology like eye in the sky (satellite photography) is assisting the production of farms and size of fish shoals. After completion of the exploration of the earth's surface, depths of the sea, unclimbed mountains, the moon and airless space are the new targets. Ocean bottom photography is exposing so far inaccessible stores of metals in the form of manganese nodules and new technologies have already mined some using special grabs sunk to the sea bottom from a surface vessel. An accessible store of metals on the moon is also a target for reaching and mining.

At this stage after thousands of years of advance of civilization, it is not easy to grasp the importance of pottery and weaving in the march of civilization. Baluchari sari is a marvel of the weaver's art. Same could also be said about Banarsi sarie woven of gold and silver threads in silk or cotton. The pottery section in any museum depicts the great contribution of the potter's wheel. Harappan abstract toys for children to complex terracotta temples of Bishnupur in Bengal are eye openers. One can only bemoan that the ancient inventor of the wheel is forgotten. Wheel has become the icon of many a god and now it even adorns the Indian national flag. Wheel is the base of communications: bullock carts, cars, trains, paddle wheels, etc. The invention of the airplane, and now jet propulsion and rockets have raised transportation to new heights. The same kind of debt, the civilization owes to the inventors of the bit, the stirrup or the nose rope for the ox. Air and water powered corn grinding mills were invented centuries ago. The invention of the steam engine and the internal combustion engine ushered in the industrial age. People have to be ambitious and confident in their need, to express the same, so that inventors and scientists can meet their needs. But if the people are contented and brain washed to live in the status quo as the gods have ordained, the invention to fill their needs will be delayed. It is prosperity and freedom that raises the demands and therefore the technological progress. Often, however, the technological advance occurs first and applications and new needs follow. Only twenty years ago in India, making a copy of a document was so laborious, Now the xerography and electronic copiers and desk top printing have become so common that everyone seems to need very often some copy or the other of a document. Perhaps the middle ages and the climate of religious contentment did not demand innovation in needs or tools. The fresh wind of reformation and discovery of new world and later the riches reaching Europe from lucrative eastern trade was the incentive to the people to express their needs and get innovative tools and instruments. For centuries, the scene was of lethargy, disease, feudal and caste or status tyranny. After the industrial revolution that started in England in the 18th century and after the experience of Company rule of India with equality before law, the floodgates of modern development occurred in Europe and India respectively. There have been important events which awakened the world to fresh goals and fresh enterprises e.g. the blocking of the forces of the Caliph at Vienna or the renaissance in Europe after the liberation of Greece from the Turkish slavery. Scientific advance began with Newton's discovery of gravity and his researches on nature of light. The reformation in Europe seemed to assist advances in mathematics. Faraday and Edison's inventions paved the way for modern living which is so much dependent on electricity. Advances in economic theory reduced the exploitation of labour. This has led to further expectation of co-operation among different classes rather than of Marxian conflict. Labour unrest is almost gone when the management is efficient and sympathetic.

Human life has been enriched by the idealists' vision of perfection and order, inventing everlasting life of the soul, inventing gods and the supreme God. The classicists enriched culture by writing songs and ballads, dramas and epics. The tedious burden of living has been eased by new technologies. Common wheel must have been invented before 3000 B.C. when Aryans invaded many parts of Asia and Africa using chariots. The inventor of scissors, needle and thread are lost from memory. Magnifying glass was used in China and India in pre-historic times. Hand tools started to be used when first man walked on two feet with hands free to grab stone or stick. Pulleys were used in ancient Egypt. Pottery advanced to great heights.

A veritable terra cotta army has been unearthed guarding a royal tomb in China. Lever was understood by Archimedes in ancient Greece. Mirrors of polished metal were used at the light-house in Alexandria in the first century B.C. From the 16th century onward there is complete record of new inventions and aids. Most of these inventions or re-inventions occurred in Europe and European colonies. The ancient builders in India used lathes to make pillars with designs. First watch was built in Switzerland in 1300 A.D. Bicycle was invented in 1816. Photography was invented in France (1826), fountain pen was invented in U.S.A. in 1860, so was electric bulb and microphone. Trade and exploitation of colonies enriched European countries so that individuals with correct inclination could pursue their inventions till they were converted to saleable items. The innovative chain could be established with ease. Twentieth century has been the century of advances in science and new technologies and the impetus is continuing. The great wars have started the bell tolling for all wars. Recent gifts of inventors are: X-ray scanner, Laser (U.S.A. 1960), Maser little earlier, Holography (Gabor-Hungary 1947), Television (Tolman and Fennworth 1923-1937 (U.S.A.), three wheeler (India 1950), Airplane (Wright Brothers, U.S.A. 1903.), Jet Aeroplane (France 1910), Echo Sounder (Canada 1914), Helicopter (France 1907), Ground cushion helicopter (India 1965-1970), Microwave oven (Spencer U.S.A.1947), Air conditioner (Carrier Co. 1902 U.S.A.), Home computer (U.S.A. 1970), ATM (Barclay's Bank U.K. 1967), tape recorder (U.S.A.). A Buddhist monk I. Hsing developed a mechanical clock in China in 720 A.D. Clock making became a European craft during the middle ages. Astronomical time keeping was begun by the astrologers of India. The contribution of the astronomers and mathematicians of India is well recorded. The Jantar Mantar at Delhi is the famous observatory in masonry built by Astronomer king of Jaipur who was in touch with astronomers of Spain and Holland. Solar and Luni-solar calendars were in vogue in various ancient civilizations. The stone-henge also was possibly an astronomical observatory built in stone in 1700 B.C.

The Establishment of the United Nations and its active agencies and panels will bring about the virtual condition of a world state allowing enough local freedom and space for local initiative. The missionary slogan of welcome to the Church since Christian nations have shown current prosperity should read that the prosperity is to be had through science, technology and innovation. There are gains in honest trade as has been seen again and again with the Quakers in England and Philadelphia, or the Jains and Marwaris in India or the Japanese, all of whom have a reputation for honest dealings.

New technologies can do wonders for more production and more prosperity. But for their successful implementation, basic qualities of truth and honesty are imperative. In India, we have had recently a glut of computers and new mobile phones. But apparently, big companies are allowing wide-spread swindling of the customer. The computer user must know that computer cannot itself cheat and will only state what it has been fed. Another firm offered internet connection to the customers at customer's cost. After few months the computer belonging to the customer, being old, failed to pick up the internet signal and the repair would have meant replacement of the computer which the customer was not prepared to do since his needs were small. When a request was made to disconnect the customer connection, the firm practically refused and month after month sent in bloated incorrect bills when the computer could not work! There are many similar complaints published in the daily newspapers. Expansion of trade and consumption cannot occur with this kind of commercial morality. One leading shaving cream distributor undertook to replace the defective item, but none of his agents ever came to do this. They announced to the local dealer when the complaint was raised by him, that the defective item has already been replaced. The basic requirement for success with new (or old) technologies is an upright character and company code of ethics overriding the malpractices of some employee or the company itself. The computer applications are unfortunately under attack from computer virus infections as well as dishonest computer familiars and thieves that cheat computer controlled payments. Computer technologists are sure to overcome most of these defects except perhaps the defect of some organization's code of conduct. A government tax collector swore that he follows exactly the tax due shown by the computer. Unfortunately, when his books were examined, they showed every entry to be revised upwards month in and month out. A general criticism of the industrial society is human alienation. The direct face to face conversation has much more social richness than the impersonal conversation through machines. The engineering system analysis used in the prosecution of all projects should be replaced by total analysis involving according to the author also the search light of logic and human values on the aims of the project. If this were done, the U.S.A. will not now be so much afraid to hurt the feelings of the Japanese after hurling atom bombs on them. To avoid future shock on not adjusting easily to future gadgetry, the firms introducing new gadgets are advised first to familiarize the public with them.

8

IDEALISM AND UTOPIA

There is always a spurt in idealism and homage to pious living after a catastrophe or a war. After the thirty years war in Europe, a German refugee in Britain (Hartlib) together with British intellectuals put forward the plea for science, liberty and a utopia. In the Mahabharata war at Kurukshetra near Delhi, the divine Krishna delivered the message of the Gita asking people to perform their duties fearlessly trusting the everlasting life for all. Thomas More's Utopia and Bacon's New Atlantic imply a welfare state for a like-minded group. Scientific romanticism was a consequence of the rational age implying a solution of all deficiencies through science. The political subordination of India to fanatics of Islam, and then to the British did not dim their faith in the freedom being their birth-right as of everyone else. When the feudal atrocities in Europe led to the French revolution, the socialist reforms gave place to dictatorship of terror, and then to the dictatorship of Napoleon. He was a reformer and a revolutionary but lived before his time. He was set on establishing an imperial dynasty and subduing the whole world with Europe as base. His dream was pursued by European imperialism. The European nations were jealous of the Spanish power in South America, Dutch power in the East Indies, and Anglo-French empires in rest of the world. Germany and Austria wanted to pull down the British empire and forced the first World War on England and France allied later with USA. The allies won a victory and sought to humiliate Germany and her allies. The Germans found a new leader in Hitler, a demagogue placing all Europe's losses at the door of the jewish rich conspiring against Christian values so dear to the Germans, a superior race of Aryans in Europe. Hitler started the second World War by attacking the weak Polish nation and massacred a million Jews in concentration camps. This was his undoing as England and USA waged a relentless war, along with the unbeaten French outside France. The axis powers lost in view of the worldwide repugnance to Nazi policies and atrocities on the defeated nations of Europe. Russian resistance to Hitler's push against them was phenomenal. After the victory of the allies, USA and Russia were left as super powers. Japan had suffered nuclear bomb attacks and was completely subdued. Its policy was to be loyal to the USA and hope to become its ally to lord over the Pacific Ocean countries according to the Japanese original war aims. India was never counted as a possible world power neglecting the inherent stamina and faith of the Indians in themselves. India was also neutralized by the setting up of Pakistan by British with American support. India was subsequently attached twice by Pakistan and once by China. Eventually with the success of Indian non-aligned policy and Russian commercial sale of sophisticated weapons and collaborative production in many industries, India could, on the third attack by Pakistan, give it a crushing defeat and then India began to be counted as possible force to reckon with in South Asia. After the Russian debacle in Afghanistan, USA became the sole super power. USA had alienated however the Muslim support in world affairs because of its anti-Palestine stance vis-à-vis Israel. USA won over Pakistan by supporting it with supply of sophisticated weapons which Pakistan was piling up for future. USA had thus purchased Pakistan's loyalty and used it as a tame elephant to win over India. India was ready having already offered non-aggression to Pakistan and had shown her willingness to discuss all outstanding matters. Thus conforming to the wishes of the super power, India and Pakistan developed their new found friendship and have celebrated the same in friendly cricket matches and almost open borders. The Islamic Jehad launched a massive terrorist attack against the USA by destroying its Trade Towers in New York and inflicting massive destruction of property and civilians. India had already been the target of the Jehadists for the prying away of the Indian border state of Kashmir. The Jehadists also were attempting to topple the dictator of Pakistan. Thus India, Pakistan and USA could afford friendship.

The opportunity to forge a charter of world peace was wasted by the Anglo-French attempt to regain their lost empires and by the Americans to form a worldwide alliance against the interests of the Soviet Union. Still a UN was set up with a Security Council with major powers having veto power. India tried to contain the cold war by suggesting an independent neutrality policy to the nations who were being enrolled in the cold war camps of USA and Russia. Russia lost in Afghan gamble and backed down when USA tried to bankrupt them by raising the level of armaments and preparations for star wars. At this juncture in the affairs of men, idealism again raised its head. The al Qaida attack on the Trade Towers in USA prompted them to revise their policy of equating India with Pakistan and first of all they brought the dictator of Pakistan into a firm alliance against Islamic Jehad targeting USA. The Indian democratic stand of eschewing any aggressive war against Pakistan convinced Pakistan that their best bargain was to be friends with India and to try to solve any mutual problems by democratic means. The slate was now clear for any re-organization of the world not to the benefit of any major power counting on the instability in Asia. The Indian policy of national freedom, support to UN and attempting to befriend all nations looked attractive to all. The internal policy of India based on secularism and assurance of human rights to all its citizens has now an appeal to all when democracy is in the ascendant.

The world is now poised for genuine co-existence for all countries and co-operation and rule of law under the aegis of the UN which is now poised for a better constitution and an expanded Security Council, along with better processes for maintenance of internal as well as external peace for all countries. The real salvation lies in speedy development all over the world and the acceptance of plurality of views in the world. With a truly democratic UN committed to global trade, global security, fight against smuggling, narcotics trade and maintenance and priority for environment being made human friendly throughout the world, the world will advance to improved health, spread of education and elimination of poverty. The humanist economics has a theorem that the poor prosper when the rich prosper. Prosperity is no longer zero-sum game with new developments in science and technology. Decentralization, autonomy and transparency will be the foundation for globalization path in production and distribution.

Idealism is summed up by Berkley that the physical world is an idea in the mind of God. What is not transparently conceivable is not logically possible. Spiritual idealism is opposed to the disintegrating forces of naturalism or of dogmatic religion. Idealism is contained in the actions as dictated by one's conscience. Through righteousness man can reach hidden mental activity and a superior understanding than what may be possible by logic alone. Intuitive knowledge cannot lead to a correct choice by itself, but it can give confirmation to a scientific or logical decision arrived at through discussion and guidance of experts. Poincare's mathematical discoveries, according to him, were primarily artistic intuitions. One invents by intuition and discusses by logic. Spiritual conduct in daily life involves identification with others. Moral education and principle of oneness with the entire human race has to be nurtured in young minds. This should mean acceptance of "Yama and Niyama". Yama is the right conduct with others and control over the six enemies viz: greed, anger, non-discrimination in right or wrong, lust, pride and jealousy. Niyama means clean living, health care, pure and simple diet, activity and orderly life. Idealism demands discipline, and faith in addition to the advanced concepts of time and space. According to Radhakrishnan, the Buddha believed that there is a deeper world of spirit penetrating the tangible world beckoning us towards righteousness. An idealist dwells on the limitations of scientific knowledge which can be overcome by enlightenment from within. Human mind is value seeking, it strives for unity and coherence which humanity should arrive at through joint and common striving.

Every religion has sought to create a utopian heaven on earth, but immediately after a brief success, decay occurred. The world cannot be restructured for few like-minded people. The answer lies in unity in diversity and co-existence. We hope to have an all embracing utopia. The best minds have to undertake education and training of the next generations. The divergences and uncertainty are basic to existence and will have to be allowed for in the constructive effort which will be spread universally. With the ability of human beings having a spread from imbecility to Buddhahood, pragmatism has to be kept up one's sleeve. The pragmatist is both idealist as well as materialist dependent on the assessment from all inputs including intuition and common sense. Since average men have to be in great majority, the values and policies must appear or be pragmatic to him. The world population is all time high, world peace has practically been achieved. The struggle now is for whole mankind to expand its living space and create better environment for sustained progress. We expect, new advances of knowledge along with gradualism will ensure a global utopia or in the phrase preferred by Young Hsieu of Korea, "Oughtopia". Man learns to be human in society. In a civilized democratic society where laws are enacted through consensus, one is to obey what is best for all. Democracy is now spreading in all corners of the world. The opportunity for social liberation is now before everyone. There is a wave of democracy even blowing in the isolated Himalayan kingdoms of Nepal and Bhutan. Even the dictatorial junta of Myanmar is waving flags of hope to the majority in opposition. Plato expected each democratic person to be loyal to himself. Social anarchy through a multitude of political and factional parties cannot be the midwife of a co-operative society. Man has a craze for domination, but society where justice and welfare are paramount can subdue this craze. Revolutionary changes are quicker according to Netaji of INA fame. In gradualism, there is no need of a step backward and the change is more certain and secure. A revolutionary change can however always overtake the gradual process. If certain reform is taking too long, it would be best to precipitate matters and gradualism so loved by idealists can be suspended. The self structure for global "Mustopia" certainty will evolve with increasing speed.

Fanaticism, howsoever irrational it may look to others, is also a kind of idealism for which the addicts are prepared to stake their lives in all kinds of mayhem including suicide so long as the fanatic can achieve damage to society. The real control of fanaticism lies in incapaciating the conspirators and the wrong kind of institutions that may have a hold on children and youth under the slogans of religion, language or personal life to be in danger of being swamped by majority inclinations. The recent outrages committed by terrorist organizations and the mafia related to Islamic *jehad* groups have become additionally virulent since they have latched on to genuine grievances of the Muslims about forced establishment of Israel in Arab Palestine in order to perpetrate cleansing of Europe from Jews. The victorious allies in World War II were carrying out the policy of Hitler in a different way. Another Islamic grievance is even more recent about the U.S. and UK aggression on Iraq. A third factor, particularly for terrorist activity against India, is the trumped up charge that India is occupying its own territory of Jammu and Kashmir where Muslims form a clear majority but this majority had rejected the embellishments of the Pakistan movement at its very inception. There are almost a billion Muslims in the world and no order of peace and community life can be established without pacification of the Muslims of the world. The world has to cut off the root of the problem which lies in the faulty education of the Muslim children supposedly by Muslim intelligentsia which is restricted to the traditional learning about Islam, shutting the mind of the students from the flow of history and advances by the world since the seventh century when Islam had its birth. The Muslim educated classes who have learnt modern science and comparative religion will have to come forward to modernize the Muslim *madrassas* to take to modern teaching of science, technology, philosophy and logic and cease brain washing to become blind followers of hate slogans. In addition the conditions in Middle East must be democratically stabilized. The Jammu and Kashmir's internal problem of this region has already been addressed by *de-facto* political partition of the state and improvements in the relations between India and Pakistan.

There can be no quarter given to the terrorists and their organizations. The narcotics trade has to be energetically suppressed since it channelizes funds to terrorist and criminal activities. Terrorists who are held by the police should be kept in educative custody till they are cleansed of the hate virus injected into them by misguided elements in their religious esteem. There should be UN-sponsored conferences for the modernization of various religions. This will help in future peaceful community life. This should not take more than a couple of centuries. Another persistent malady is that of corruption. If the administration in government or private organizations is efficient, corruption is minimized by transparency in decision making. The children must be taught to reform their elders, since the stock alibi of the corrupt is that they indulge in corruption to give a better standard of life to their families and children. The Chinese cultural revolution has some lessons for such teaching. The volunteers who successfully fight corruption should be given special privileges including "national service medals". Terrorism must be fought with the firmness of truth and justice and not by counter-terrorism.

9

MIGHT IS RIGHT

The times have changed. In the past humility was considered an important virtue, but humility as a virtue was meant for those who had the wealth or knowledge or power and not for the common man. The net result was that the common man first was humble only before lords and gods, and then he was humbled by higher castes and the well-to-do. The proud sought more power and kings went about seeking and robbing fellow kings of their kingdoms. For most of mankind's history, 'might is right' was the principle most honoured by all. Humility and human rights stayed in the books of religion, and have gained general attention only now when the wars have practically become outlawed and rule of law nationally or internationally is in sight. In place of resolving disputes that arose, by patience, discussion and flexibility or resort to legal remedies, the most direct way was considered to be a resort to arms. The dispute was regarded as an opportunity for the two armed camps of the disputants. The claims and counter-claims never died down but the tension simmered to break out again now here and now there. History of the world has been history of wars to resolve disputes, wars of outright invasion for the expansion of real estate, war over land of totally innocent strangers, wars of succession, wars to impose unwelcome trade or wars to support gun-boat diplomacy etc., etc. Among the foreign invasions, the notorious are the nomadic invasions in Eurasia, Mongol and Japanese invasions of China, Arab and Turkish tribal invasions of India, Thai invasions of Cambodia, Burma and India, French invasion of England and *vice versa*. The build up of the Austro-Hungarian empire, the Greek or the Roman empires, the European empires of the last couple of centuries, Arab rape of Africa culminating in the slave trade, European violence in spreading the blessing of modern advances in both the Americas. The worse culprits have been the urges to have empires and to violently spread Islam and Christianity, both these religions had been revealed to promote peace and brotherhood. The two world wars of the twentieth century were fought ostensibly for liquidating the Anglo-French empires or for ending the threat of enslavement from fascist dictators of Germany, Italy or Japan. A strange war fought in diplomacy was the cold war to end world wide web of dictatorships theorized by communism and boiled down to dictatorship of Stalin or Mao-tze-tung. It is the stress of the cold war that convinced the world that peace is the best policy, and the leaders and people everywhere began piling up powers and responsibilities on the United Nations which now is the last hope of mankind for peaceful possession of the planet earth till doomsday. The sincerity of the world powers in this is still shaky. Many a voice seems to feel nostalgia for imperial peace in sections under the heel of an empire and talk hopefully of the supremacy of a single super power to preside over "peaceful" progress in the world. The sooner they realize, the better it would be that human mind is so constructed, being full of good and evil, that without decentralization and giving people freedom in exercise of their rights and the choice of avenues of success in their local efforts, the peace will be a chimera. A considerable effort in education and ground preparation for the unity of the world has to be mounted for winning the minds of the people. To guard the human possession of the earth, a way has to be found to free people from crazy politicians chasing their petty ambitions and partial utopias and to rid the earth from wars and rebellions.

It is futile to wait for the entire mass of people to think

alike. We have to spread the philosophy of acceptance and co-existence. God as well as atheist's belief in goodness and socialism have all to be used in this restructuring of thought. UN is on the right track, without aiming at a world state and world government, it seeks assurance of faithful exercise of human rights by all, co-operation among nations and strengthening the UN for performing many international tasks assigned to it. International law must be established by agreement and enforced by the UN. Lone furrows by ambitious persons or individuals would become counter-productive and success in co-operation should emerge as the best option. Indian policies of co-existence and co-operation are good example to other large and small countries. India is experimenting with preserving her growth through recognizing legitimate interests of her neighbours. India is totally against minority bashing or ethnic cleansing. It is committed to secularism. All laws are framed through discussion, love and logic. The only problems that bedevil Indian progress arise from continuing corruption in government departments and its spread in private industry primarily from inefficiency in administration and in the selection of human tools. There is perhaps a need of forging a special task force equipped with own publicity and television channel to fight corruption by means of special investigation techniques and access to official documents. India has never committed and will never commit an aggression within or outside India. It believes in progress through democratic discussion. The ongoing globalization of production and trade will increase prosperity in all countries if there is vigilance against in-efficiency and procrastination. Slowly many international or UN agencies will take over the problems of food, environment and security. World can aim to become a *de facto* world state by intelligent co-operation of people and of nations. The new governance will encompass the whole world. Indians believe and have faith in the dictum that truth shall prevail. In evidence they trot out many prison sentences awarded by the courts to the high and mighty for corruption in India. However, at present bullying of the weak and aggrandizement of the strong seems to be having an easy time.

The real answer to the might cannot be counter force which only prolongs the aggression and the counter steps. The effective counter force of justice i.e. love has to be applied. Love and non-violence are the teachings of Christ and Gandhi. If violence and injustice continue, anarchy would lead to the Biblical prediction that the meek shall inherit the earth and the earth may be hardly recognizable from a graveyard or a picture of devastation. It is the united will of the people that topples tyrants and dictators. The realization that the new revolution is not being engineered by a miracle worker or leader of a sect, class or a mob, but by the convinced great majority of people as expressed by their chosen representatives and through the co-operation of nation states who are slowly building the governance of the whole world through the organs and policies as adhered to in the UN. It is unfortunate that an agent of the UN has taken the bit in its teeth and violently subdued the independent existence of Iraq. This must be the last flicker of defective international gun boat diplomacy so dear to imperialists and quasi imperialists. The world has already travelled far on the global path and the imperialists hiding behind the veil of altruistic riches will also soon come to heel. Already they are swearing by a united Iraq which like other nations will be a willing member of the UN and forget the bad dream of violence perpetrated on it. The injustice borne by Iraq will strengthen the democratic solution of Israel's existence and Palestinian emergence as a full fledged nation. Nations both strong and weak have equal rights in the UN system of governance by co-operation and efficient deployment of resources in the interest of the entire world. Middle East has been the crossroads of the world. This geographical status is unalterable. An important aspect of the ongoing globalization will be close friendly regional relationship of these countries bordering the Mediterranean Sea and the Red Sea. Dual membership of these countries in other regional groupings like the European Union or the African Union or SAARC will be authorized by the affected regional bodies. The Middle East

Union will have an important role in world governance of energy and air communications and most important of all in the continued peace and development also in the Balkans and the horn of Africa. This will also bury for good the needless discontentment between Iraq and Iran all so well endowed by nature and centuries long prosperity as world leaders.

The ghost of the Persian saying that "..Pidram Sultan bood" i.e., my forefathers were kings has to be dismissed from the memory of the new generation and new prosperity will make them welcome the new dispensation. The General Assembly will have to soon pass a resolution asking the USA to again swear allegiance to the UN in view of the presidential remark that they cannot brook any equal in the UN. The UN has been organized vowing equality of all nations and same human rights for all world citizens. Only the veto is continuing as a bye-product of recent history. The peace and development in the world will be little affected by the existence of the veto when in due course the General Assembly shows human wisdom controlling human folly. The international community has to use the present period for enunciating international law in bits to be adopted by the General Assembly within next couple of years. Rule of law will be the best guarantee for continued progress so essential for making the world a fit home for humanity for eternity. Rule of law will also tackle the nuisance of terrorism, trade in narcotics and exploitation of weaker sections including women and children. An insurance against future revolts and wars will be placing all disputes on the consultation front burner of the UN for nipping any growing strife in the bud. A welfare state devoid of an agenda for human development will only be an environment of suffocation as already seen in colonial attempt at spreading religion and civilization that suited the imperialists.

Education for peace and promotion of a culture of human development in peace should start immediately with the promise that in the next few centuries, a world citizenship spreads globally in assurance of security of self, personal property, speedy redressal of complaints and exercise of universal human rights. Only legitimate might will be right as determined by the international law and world citizenship.

Criminals resort to terrorism and must be handled by the police. Fanatics and brain-washed extremists are of a different kind. The terrorism by criminals will have to be met by firm action by the police. For the brain-washed kind of terrorism of the fanatics, those that may escape immediate reprisals by the police or the military but are nabbed, they should be placed in a special hospital-cum-lunatic-asylum for rehabilitation. If enquiries reveal that fanatics of a particular kind are created in certain special schools, all such schools must be declared illegal and must stay closed. Mahatma Gandhi also endorsed the use of violence by convinced defenders against bullies and criminally inclined fanatics. Mindless terrorism is a recent occurrence in USA, UK, Egypt and India which is due to the fanaticism of the discontented Muslims. The world has to take note of the mischief being caused by the current interpretation of *jehad.* The Islamic *madrassas* should be enjoined to impart instruction in science and modern ideas of astronomy and evolution. The entire human race is poised at the threshold of everlasting progress and peace. To avoid any social strife, every nation should have workable personal law legally allowing certain exceptions in view of tenacity of traditional customs, but the goal of uniform personal law should be kept for future and it can be achieved in a century or two. Terrorism has been recognized as cancerous in the modern world. There is a requirement of a world wide vigil against its appearance anywhere so that any low key spread does not take place.

10

SCIENCE AND TECHNOLOGY

Science has been with us from the very beginning when man learnt the relation between cause and effect. The complexity of time can be dealt with only when experimenting with fundamental particles or with astronomical ages and distances. Science rests on seeking truth from experience and experimentation. The distinctive feature of science is that all its theories are tentative like in Jain philosophy. A theory is jettisoned if it does not explain what it should have or a new observation requires a better theory to cover it. The scientists are happy in expanding the coverage of their concepts and in the process the concepts are improved. Science also has no impassable barriers. Its frontiers are always receding. Heaven is supposed to be an ever lasting place of sheer joy where there is continuous hum of praises being sung of the Lord. Science will have nothing to do with such a place. For science the existence must be on the move. If by utopia we want heaven on earth, this heaven must have room for science. Humanity assured of peace will still be active in promoting happiness by spreading more culture and riches among the people. There will exist further frontiers of science to be crossed. Some forgotten truths as well as old observations will have to be reassessed and the forgotten worker again remembered as was done in case of Galileo. The science of economics and science of biology have to advance till the mechanics of creative evolution is properly understood. Space travel, so far a dream, has to be realized. During preparations new sciences of the brain may develop and new kind of humanity evolve giving further meaning to human eternity. Dwindling material resources and living space per person will require lot of science and technology to make up the shortfall. Artificial insemination has improved livestock. Such technology and further developments in stem cell researches may be applied in a controlled manner to improve human beings. Education pills have yet to be invented. The "Puranic" (Hindu mythological) fiction speaks of instantaneous transfer of long texts to the pupils. So far there is only fragmentary knowledge about the functioning of the brain or the complexity of the three dimensional structure of the bio-molecules and their importance to life. The subjects of biology, use of bio-molecules for specialized computers are practically hidden in the future. The current revolution in information technology promises great increase in production at less cost and for less expenditure of energy. Energy availability has to be increased. Nuclear energy limited by the facilities for the disposal of waste products can double the present production of electricity. There is almost limitless scope from the energy availability from the thermal gradient in the oceans and the problem there is of building off-shore electric supply stations and preferably using the supply in close by off shore industrial factory ships for fish processing and canning or metallic electrolytic processing factories, etc if the manganese nodules are being hauled up from the sea bottom near by. These works will require century of peace time effort and we have many such centuries to spare.

Centuries of effort still needed to focus on mental telepathy and television without instrumental aids, to make it reliable at least for some minds. Automation will develop still further and the railways may overcome the occasional collisions and derailments. Here is going to be enough work for scientists and technologists for all time. Every such development will give birth to many applications. The world will be assured of expansion of remunerative jobs for all. In any case, new capitalism and socialism will converge through new humanist economics to provide life long sustenance wage to everyone. Remunerative work will only bring additional income for spending on increased production and availability of all kinds of merchandise in the globalized market place reaching out to everyone.

In a peaceful and prosperous world, there will be expansion of travel and entertainment, good food and environmental control. Scientific advances are necessary in the forecasting of weather and extrapolation of all kinds of data. Designer clothes will be available for everyone and world wide fashions will come in vogue. Medical sciences will converge on assuring people of good health perhaps through exhortation for the classical simple living and naturopathy. Spare human limbs, from voluntary donors or from substitute materials will be readily available. Everyone will have normal eyesight either natural or assisted by medical and opticians help. New technologies using molecular semi-conduction and bio-molecules will miniaturize the computer no end giving immense boost to human enterprise and creativity. Practically life like and special capability robots will be developed for inaccessible places and difficult tasks beyond the capability of human beings. Objective testing of human aptitudes and talents as well as character will be begun and this may involve a month's stay with chosen experts. The effort will be worthwhile if it promotes early recognition of a genius and fertile brain not to be wasted in wrong tasks. It is incorrect to honour achievement primarily on the basis of caste, creed or region. All awards should be freed from such undemocratic overriders. But in the interest of backward groups and regions special coaching funds should be provided for the promising young men from those categories. An organization in England or USA selects awardees for all kinds of high sounding awards, but such awardees can be collected only by the rich as the cost of the award certificate is prohibitive except for the well to do. For an ordinary citizen their award is almost a punishment. The awards policy of the national governments needs further scrutiny and require a court of appeal since these are covered often by influence peddling by less than honest "leaders" of science of these countries especially where independent editors of scientific journals are missing. We are not sure how a wavelet is first produced on a smooth sheet of water. We would like to know how a fresh thought is formed in the human mind. The experiments on parapsychology can lead nowhere unless specially capable brains are first selected. Our ambition would be to pinpoint the parapsychological capability of everyone. In our long future we may have to draw on such capability during space travel or research in difficult spaces like the polar regions or water depths.

Psychologists could be supported to carry out research on dreams (and dreamed ambitions). Can we induce sleep in a subject just so that he can, when awake, report on his dreams and the researcher can correlate it with other simultaneous happenings or report of possible connected happenings as given by the subject. Brains of identical twins might be of some assistance in this as how they converge and diverge. In fact, brain research is in infancy and may take a few centuries to bear fruit. A child once refused to close his eyes at sleeping time, saying that he wants to sleep with eyes open, so that he can see his dreams more clearly! Perhaps dream research can lead to some key about the future imbecility or the creative talent of a subject. The eternity of humanity is likely to last at least till the earth continues to be livable i.e., for another two billion years.

Every new technology creates new jobs, new comforts and greater satisfaction in life. For the results to be availed, necessary infrastructure has to be in place. With the revolution in electronics by the invention of semi-conductor devices and their applications, the markets are bulging with electronic goods for the customers. But in India, the acute shortage of electrical power makes it difficult even to demonstrate the performance of these devices. Microchip manipulation has reduced the size of the electronic devices especially of computers and made them cheaper to suit the pockets of ordinary citizens. Digitally recorded music is now in every household. Television channels have increased a great deal. One can choose special channels catering to a particular kind of entertainment or information. Greater number of channels and choice of programmes without aimless scrolling over channels would be possible. Laser operations have made removal of opacity in the eye an out patient affair without any hospitalization. Invention of machine operated medical diagnosis and treatment have made it easy for patients. Computers have made visits to banks redundant provided the banks faithfully feed correct data to the computer. Tax collecting can be made less painful, except that the tax offices have occasionally to be checked that they have good records to back up the computer and not records with too many corrections and over-writings. New technical achievements have been used in remote sensing, and telemetry. These help in resource exploration and management of value addition in agriculture, forestry, and fodder availability, location of forest fires, or help in human migrations on the occurrence of a natural disaster.

Materials technology has provided newer materials not only replacing old ones but with new designed molecules prone to new applications, especially in the area of polymers and elastomers or electrets and magnetic materials. Human ingenuity is wonderful, without modern aids, the architects and builders of yore built such wonders as the Taj, the pyramids, the hanging gardens of Babylon, the Great Wall of China, Angkor Vat of Cambodia, reclaimed sea bottom as land for farming in Holland etc. With new materials and machines, man can accomplish much more. The latest wonder in Delhi is the new metro. Already every city in India is hoping to have one. This alone will open new workshops and jobs in every large city. It would be possible in the world where money will be forthcoming for investment if the project is going to be profitable or fulfilling an urgent need. I am looking for the day when a robot secretary could be easily persuaded for day-to-day assistance to the citizen to keep his affairs in order, to keep advertisers at bay and be his private memory for social affairs, sorting out the messages and letters that are received unendingly. Not in a too distant future, say in the next millennium, flying apartments will be available for parking at stations dotted all over the scenic world for adding zest and zeal to sight seeing and entertainment. Urban design will undergo a revolution. The urban apartments will be designed as suitable for a small practically self contained population of about ten thousand souls, and the towns will have vehicle entry exit only at fixed hours while for rest of the day, most of the town streets will be open only for those travelling on foot, bicycles or in carts pulled by hand or some machine at a maximum speed of ten miles per hour. Most of the streets will have grass lawns with tiny cart paths on each side. Metros will serve broadly a square of 100×100 square kms. and do all the heavy load ferrying either below ground or on fenced or elevated tracks. The towns will function like autonomous villages of old. There will be capital cities and ports at suitable locations for special administration and business activities. This kind of materialization will take couple of millennia of the peaceful future.

Some of the knowledge is basically global, like geography, archaeology, environment, agriculture, oceanography, seismology, glaciation, volcanology, soil science, physics and chemistry of the atmosphere, etc. etc. International co-ordination has already started in such areas through the concerned international associations and the specialized agencies of the UN. This is a readymade aspect of the future world governance. Law of the sea has been framed by democratic procedure and most countries already adhere to the same. Space exploration might begin with the moon. According to the theory advanced by the author, the moon has been assembled around a metallic disc expelled in the atomic explosion that occurred in the earth about four billion years ago. As a proof, the oldest rocks on the earth and on the moon will have a sizeable difference in age. The metallic disc embedded in the moon will be easily accessable for mining and this might be a welcome resource for the earth in view of depletion of metallic ores on the earth. More advances are expected within the current century in the production of thermonuclear power, charge transfer complexes, fungal metabolites, explosive welding, biological studies in vitro, stem cell research. For quickening the pace of research, more resources of education and instruments have to be spared for it. We suggest the institution of world wide fellowships that would disseminate the expertise widely. Certain life-long fellowships are needed for support to creative genius. The recipient will be selected by the recognized great in any area of science and technology.

Certain subjects are only now shedding their lethargy and seizure by individualism like economics, history and philosophy and useful results are now expected. The reconstruction of human society in the proper direction of world society of culture and peace will involve intensive attention to values, secular approach and education of children as well as continuing education of professionals.

The importance of international familiarity and collaboration in certain fields strikes anyone. The subjects like astronomy, ecology and molecular biology are obviously subjects of choice for world-wide attention of planners. A break through in agriculture, and longevity with better health is now visible in gene studies and its applications. Many international joint teams and collaborating institutions are on the job. The research, if they start involving competent and learned people of less developed countries, might provide more resources of men and materials in advancing such fields of work. International projects of astronomical observation and theory and instrumented satellite and observation platforms, need to be launched in space. Giant energy and distilled water plants need to be established world wide. International research has to be globally coordinated in many emerging fields e.g. Giant telescopes, and *nano-meter* microscopes, thermal energy from the sea, chelates and charge transfer complexes, impact extrusion, ultra pure metals, instruments for ocean fish estimation, astro-biology, plant cell biology, fluorescence imaging technology, international law and model personal law etc, etc.

Such a tremendous effort will now be possible since warlike researches indulged by most developed countries can be diverted to human development researches.

10.1 ORIGIN OF LIFE AND EVOLUTION OF HUMAN BEINGS

Oparin (1924) held that chemical evolution preceded the evolution of life. The primeval atmosphere of earth contained traces of H_2, CH_4, ammonia, water and formaldehyde HCHO. These substances occur in the cosmic space too. In the presence of large amounts of energetic radiation, formation of a large number of organic molecules in the reducing atmosphere followed. Some amino-acids, some sugars and some other compounds have been detected in ancient rocks. Volcanism could contribute to the formation locally of monomers. This was the emergence of order from chaos. Proteinoids with catalytic properties were soon formed. These were the biological precursors of cells. The switch to biological evolution is associated with the origin of the genetic code through the catalytic reaction of the poly-nucleotides and poly-peptides. The autocatalysis etc. occurred in the Darwinian system. There is a system bound limit of transfer of information of 10^{17} bits. For propagating more complex systems, use was made of emerging sex and of genetic recombination. There was an explosive evolution of cell organelles in the switch from prokaryotes to eukaryotes (first single cell algae). The chemical evolution began about 4 billion years ago and continued for another two and a half billion years upto the formation of present day atmosphere of the earth but the evolution picked up speed afterward when a symbiotic relation between the aerobic and anaerobic cells began. Cell differentiation, growth of cells and morphogenesis occur by a genetic programme. Active movement of cells is stimulated by molecular signalling. In the later stages of development hormones begin to operate. The specific presence of cell differentiation is responsible for immunity e.g. for the production of anti-bodies in the organism of the vertebrates. The immune system protects the organism from the harmful effects of microorganisms.

The biological development both ontogenesis and phylogenesis progresses in the direction of increasing complexity and the information value is increased. Rapid evolution based on neural mutation slightly reduces adaptation. Systems of high complexity possess in principle the ability to produce more complexity than they have themselves. This might offer some hope that evolution could produce further capabilities of the human brain. The change of a genome is associated with the entire evolution process. An understanding of the genome has been pursued to suggest ways of inducing evolutionary improvement in the human brain.

It is the mutation of the gene that takes an organism from one path to another. In society transformation, a general burst of innovation acts as a mutation. With the growth of science and technology and global activation of youth, the transformation of society in the forward direction will be expected soon and the human beings and their society have to be watchful that the advances are welcome and which can be built upon further. The evolution theory therefore extends hope that both human beings and human society are on the verge of some desirable mutation. Much more wherewithal must be spared for biological and cybernetic work in view of the estimated improvements. An instinctive abhorance of violence could arise.

The optimism regarding the viability of the human genome after a billion years from today depends on the continued advances in biology with a watch on the future mutations and genome manipulation for keeping to the track of human identity.

11

HUMANIST ECONOMICS

Along with creative evolution, economics needs a little push to become humanist as advocated by Prof. Amartya Sen, welfare, economics is inclined towards socialist interest in the equitable distribution of wealth between the rich and the poor. Humanist economics alone can look after the Sarvodaya of Mahatma Gandhi resulting in a smile on the face of the poorest of the land. Welfare economics has an undertone of charity and discriminatory dole for the poor. The dole is so much looked down upon that the poor associate it with the destiny of a beggar. So much so that they may like to sponge on the friends and relations than register for dole as unemployed and poor. To remove this derogatory association, the humanist economic makes an estimate of the living wage that can meet the Maslow needs of an individual with one dependent. The economy distributes this wage or maintenance allowance to each adult above 18 years of age without any enquiry into his/her financial and property ownership status. Those who are willing to receive this amount each quarter will also undertake to contribute manual or clerical labour as direct by the national labour and employment board for atleast eight hours (distributed over each week). In case they can do some required work for longer period, they will be entitled to the hourly wage rate for the extra period. Every adult will be entitled to a rent free residence comprising one room and one toilet. His work place will as far as possible be within one km. of his residence. This alone will cover the minimum responsibility of the state for welfare of its citizens.

Man is greedy and acquisitive by nature. From the experience of dole in affluent countries and grains for labour schemes in India, this scheme also will need careful supervision and accounting for the money and the labour involved. The eye and ears of the government will be active in the Panchayats and the schemes will be decentralized to the district level. All governments will have learnt how the dishonest officials frustrate ameliorative measures by quietly pocketing the outlays that have to reach the people and also the measures taken to defeat such crimes. Since each adult is bracketed with one dependant, the problem of sustenance needs of most children and destitute elders will also be solved. The district officer will also be the controller of all charities including charitable funds collected or accumulated by the religious places of worship or religious groups. Any excessive load of children will be looked after from the charity funds by the district officer in consultation with appropriate NGO's and religious charities who will democratically select an advisory panel in this regard. All charities and charity boxes at temples and religious places will be under the control of the district officer.

In the forgotten mists of antiquity, there was communal life of the tribe with the family elder as the supreme authority. But with the yea and nay nature of human beings, it would not last. Soon private property and exclusive right to it became the driving force for human activity and the growth of human civilization. The society got fed up with the "might is right" thinking and the deeds of feudal lords, dictators and the dictation of capital-finance. Communism was tried in Paris, Russia and China with big expectations, but everywhere it ended up in dictatorship of one leader, terrorism and factionalism. The only lasting communism is the communism of the Indian Marxists wedded to Indian democracy so much so that India might become a communist country with parliamentary democracy. China is already a communist country with pragmatic policies both internal and external. National development needs will be met with the willing work of scientists, technologists and labour. The doctrinnaire fiats will not take the economy far especially in present times when the happenings in one place are immediately known in another. Comparisons are easily made and the standard of living and earning of an average worker in U.S.A. and some rich countries of Europe and Asia are far above the present earnings in China or Cuba or West Bengal run by parliamentary communism within the central rule at Delhi of the centrist parties.

When India became free in 1947, it had already started the exercise in planning economic development and an all round restructuring of society. Nehru, the architect of modern Indian state, introduced an emphasis on secularism, and inter-communal peace and friendship, a foreign policy of co-existence even with Pakistan who had opted for a policy of confrontation and territorial aggrandizement at the cost of India with declared policies of friendship with all countries, of non-violence and disarmament. Nehru launched the mixed economy as the pragmatic economic doctrine, but his detractors called him a fellow-traveller. The communists came around to fighting elections and came to power in two Indian states. The majority of states did not vote communism and did better with the mixed economy than the communist-run states. The Indian situation was made miserable by the machinations of thwarted imperialism. The British created Pakistan as a thorn in the flesh of India. It is still trying to wrench a part of India under threats of Islamic Jehad. For a number of years U.S.A. coddled it for possible use in the Middle East and against Indian aspirations. Pakistan continued in its posture of an aggrieved weak nation, but started two wars of aggression against India for forcing the detachment of its J&K state. India believed in resolving all disputes by peaceful discussion and a policy of flexibility. After India had demonstrates its resolve to defend itself and the success of its economic performance, the dissolution of the Soviet Union, and a new reassessment of the world situation, India and Pakistan have decided to live in peace and as loyal members of the UN. Indian policy of non-alignment was the refuge of all freedom loving nations when there was cold war. India's policy was to be friends with all nations and to co-operate in every way with the United Nations where India is all for reorganization of the UN and also a candidate for a permanent seat in the Security Council. It is now member of the four well-off nations who are in the forefront with the proposal for reorganization of the UN. USA and the UN also have expressed themselves for restructuring of the UN and the Veto. UN and the world are getting converted to greater role of the UN agencies in the governance of the world for economic progress and peace. India and Pakistan are now in cohorts to make a success of SAARC which will soon move to form a common market.

The mixed economy places considerable trust in efforts to eradicate poverty by investing in research and training of human resources. The policy of peaceful co-operation and speedy eradication of differences would soon provide for the Maslow needs and psycho-social needs of education, training and mobility as well as recreation. All will be assured of equal rights and equal status. This will remove the present disaffection with caste assigned status. For increasing production and decreasing costs, more trust will be placed, on entrepreneurs and their skill in setting up economical production and new profitable manufactures as well as addition of industrial or management values. The national wealth does not exist just in GDP or in bank vaults, but most of it is in the expertise and in the capability of its citizens.

The prosperous nations are on trial in the new regime of globalization of market if they take agreed measures to increase trade by less protection against imports and reasonable prices on exports. Free trade must limit subsidies beyond reason for home production. There should be reciprocal respect for intellectual property of all nations. Traditional ways of using materials automatically confers property rights and need not be buttressed by patents by the nation owning the tradition or these are not to be superceded by ignorant patents issued elsewhere. It has been proposed by many an author that the revamped UN should have an Economic Security Council also coordinating the WTO and national economics. The economic progress will universalize democracy and human rights in all countries. The exports will have to match the imports which will have to increase with the provision of more spending power with the poor in the humanist economics. Relatively poor countries will have to set store with simplicity in life style, some relief will be here as less money may have to be kept apart for import of costly weapons in new world of peace and progress. Panglossian expectation, that natural and competitive processes lead to optimum results, does not hold either in biology or in economics. The evolutionary analogies do not hold for economics since there can be no inherited traits. But bursts of innovation, it is believed, will act as mutation of genes! It becomes necessary to develop the innovative skills for the success of the humanist economics.

Lessons learnt from the great depression, we are sure, have not been forgotten. Both too much money flowing in or going out are bad for health of an economy. Stagflation has to be kept out by providing funds for new technologies and conversion training looking to the future well ahead. Prof. Indiresan has contributed lot of economic common sense for treating economic maladies. Poor must get above the poverty line. It is not necessary to worry about the rich getting richer. The society is constituted by both the rich and the poor. For efficient government spending, red tape of pre-audit only slows down the aimed progress. Post-audit should be prompt and concerned feed back that may arise must be used for correction of future spending. For vitality of the economics, credit has to expand and red-tape must be cut down including employment of unnecessary staff. For increase in agricultural wages, agro-industries could be set up in rural blocks. Large mechanized farms are suitable when man-power is limited and farm production is for neighbouring large scale industry of special nature. High consumption by the public will stimulate economy and is all right if inflation can be kept at bay by controlling the interest rates. If aggregate demand is deliberately restricted, recession can be created, but a certain slack in economy will combat inflation. Inheritance law should be so applied that productive farms or factories do not become less efficient. If there is no proper heir, the factory or means of production should be taken over by the state at first for three years and then if necessary handed over to a competent co-operative or sold to a private owner.

12

EDUCATION

Education and training are the tools with which human material is to be driven to constructive channels that will bring about the universal brotherhood, a utopia covering the entire human race. The goal is very much practical and reachable now that war has practically been outlawed and is no tactic for any nation's extraordinary goals or ambitions. UN has been established with many international councils for specific tasks. Security Council is now the subject of democratic debate and an agreed revision of the structure of the UN and its Security Council is around the corner. With a reasonable future of planned progress, acceptance at large of humanist economics and perseverance in scientific and technological advance, the mankind will assure itself an eternity of existence. For all this the human beings themselves have to get adequate education and training. Remunerative employment will be available to all and for this everyone must receive education and training. Every individual has a distinctive personality, aptitudes and talents which have to be allowed to come out when one is very young. The psychologists will be developing test batteries for this. Those who have family involvement in some cottage industry, a suitable profession or trade, should if found fit, be encouraged to get the education and training while engaged in the family profession. Lot of knowledge can be imparted by the medium of a wage earning job. Primary education would be compulsory while high school education could be completed in broken periods interrupted by other interests and work experience of the student. Each high school graduate will be assigned to a tutor, who will look after his ward's growth till a new tutor is selected by the ward. Teachers and tutors should be such as are satisfied with their ordinary standard of life but are proud of their status in society which gives them due honour. I discovered society finds ways to give honour to research workers. In USA, when I wanted to have my old car repaired, a garage undertook to repair it at half the usual cost since I was a Carnegie research fellow. Similarly a shopkeeper in Tokyo on his own reduced the price of an article I required 20 per cent since he found that I was a scholar and the guest of their society for the promotion of science. At the childhood stage proper values can be instilled in children by competent teachers and knowledgeable loving parents. Special efforts are needed to educate the poor and backward class youth regarding their rights, democratic equality and opportunities waiting for them, about educational loans and insurance or bank loans. Hypocrites among teachers or parents cannot guide them effectively. Healthy, ethical and moral values are essential even superior to asceticism, "bhakti" or prayers. The purveying of trash programmes on radio and television has to cease. The programme channels can be in large numbers so that specific channel can be selected for the edification and additional knowledge of anyone. Entertainment for both children as well as adults should have an uplifting quality. The values of secularism and work culture have to be inculcated by both precept and example. Education should excite and satisfy natural curiosity of the student as recommended by Prof. Feynman and by Tagore. In the learning of history, a discussion of the reasons for a particular event may be more instructive than the date of its occurrence. If a proper opportunity presents itself, an average student who had shown no special ability might begin to shine in the proper line of work. One dropout bully became later a great expert on wild animals and was adviser to zoos of the country. For the development of entire world in the society for eternity, all kinds of men and women can contribute and all must receive loving care and education. Higher institutes of learning should be residential with dedicated teachers and even dedicated technicians since skills can also best be learnt in youth. A Japanese teaching workshop was asking the children to develop a machine that can walk on a dozen legs! Famous universities like Oxford and Cambridge have eminent professors living in the university to have an eye on students with quality and inquisitiveness. Considerable responsibility rests on journals of advanced learning as they are responsible for creating or marring many reputations sometimes without adequate reason. The refereeing of intellectual product cannot be done mechanically as yes or no and deserves much more attention and constructive effort.

By the next millennium, the problem of choosing the right profession for anyone would have been solved by expected new brain mapping techniques. Further advance in humanism and human aspirations might create a new type of human being that can do away with the need of a government maintaining order in society as predicted in the communist doctrine. It is conflict resolution that brings about the advanced philosophical structure of stable change. Young Seek Choue emphasizes that the aim now is the restructuring of society and to establish governance in the emerging multipolar world. People have to be educated to aspire for the common society. Complex interdependence binds all human beings. Youth must be encouraged to take on value related tasks. Fostering of goodwill and friendship means sincerity in one's promises. Promotion of world culture includes the promotion of regional co-operation. All suggestions for improvement require sincere consideration. Sustainable ideal development effective even for the poorest of the poor (Sarvodaya according to Gandhi) means balanced and integrated development. Mahatma Gandhi disapproved of faulty means to reach faultless goal. Mr. Annan, the UN Secretary-General, opines "Current globalization of market is driven by global elite". What is required is progress with justice. Globalization of market has as seen from performance data caused some unemplcyment which ought to be compensated with increase of entrepreneurship and this can be facilitated. More production alone can give enough to all.

For uplift of the down trodden, they themselves have to start thinking differently. They must not regard their poor state as just for their deeds in this or some earlier life. World can and will be reorganized to give everybody a chance to participate in the coming life of plenty. Even at the height of caste rigidity in India, some men of grit became universally respected sages or saints like Namdev (a tailor), Tukaram (a farmer), Raidas (a cobbler), Raskhan and Kabir (working class Muslims). Adherence to morality of truth, non-violence and celibacy outside wedlock is important for success in revolutionizing society to one of world culture and progress. Friendships and fellow feeling alone can bring races and different philosophies together. As a preparation for global society, the education has to be free, mandatory and non-sectarian. Strict control has to be placed on religious schools. The religious schools could train the priests in the rituals prescribed by all religions at births, deaths, etc. so that the same priest can give service to followers of all religions who desire rituals. Teachers must know local language and local events for picking up rapport with children. The teaching should include the teaching of an international language besides one or two common languages including the mother tongue of the majority of the children in that class. The *madrassa* type education has shown success in producing fanatics. Perhaps it can be adopted for creating children crusaders against corruption as was demonstrated in the early stages of the cultural revolution in China.

The vocation of becoming a teacher should be as attractive as any other calling or profession. After school education people who chose teaching should enroll in a training college for teachers and learn the art and science of teaching for at least three years. Those who train teachers must be dedicated souls to the profession. Non-teaching staff should also be a contented lot and be selected carefully as they can undo much of the good work of the institution by treating the students shabbily. Teachers should be taught to give the students also physical training, introduction to music and group singing, public speaking, etc along with other extracurricular activities. It should be dinned into them that they will be the creators of citizens of the new world of achievement and direct affinity with other fellow citizens of the world.

The Indian classification at birth is totally out of date. The society now believes in equal rights, reason and justice, equal opportunity, flowering of one's ability and special talents if any. The education is not simply grading of people but it is for self-actualization and progress. The work culture is to be propagated. Training by allotting tasks and problems to be solved, writing essays along with other fellow students, all towards imbibing the habit of self help and reference work in the library etc. will assist the pupil to perform creative work and research in any field. Teachers have to encourage their pupils to welcome and to excite curiosity in the topic being taught. The pupils have to be guided into good reading, to be punctual and interested in the activity of the world around them. According to the Bhrigu's (an ancient Indian seer) code, a youth who habitually reveres the elders, progresses in four things: reputation, knowledge, fame and strength. According to the Vedas, austerity, self-control, earnestness and meditation are the foundation of knowledge.

Colleges and universities should be interlinked so that instruction in a new field can progress even when there is paucity of experts as teachers.

12.1 VALUE EDUCATION AND SECULAR APPROACH

The important preparations for a world of security and well-being are the inculcation in young minds of importance of value education and of secular approach. Value education has been accepted by the UNESCO as a constructive measure and they have recognized an NGO "World Association of Value

Education" which has branches in many countries. The basis of value education is now included in the syllabus of any teachers training college. It is the cherished values that help one discriminate between right and wrong. Certain values are regarded as part of human nature and can be used as the distinguishing feature of human beings. Humanism thus includes love of truth, forgiveness, hospitality, charity, recognition of duties and of human rights. Values determine worth-while goals. The most important goal before humanity now is the establishment of a community of peace and progress in the whole world. Since man is a complex personality and all humanity cannot be expected to hold same views, the goal therefore is to achieve unity in diversity and to establish a democratic system of governance where everyone is conscious of his/her freedom as well as duties and responsibilities as a world citizen. This cannot come about by a monolithic world government or authorized world view. But it is easy if man accepts the value of love and friendship, a disposition to listen and to discuss and not seeking converts but accepting coexistence of variety of thought since it is the variety that will ensure progress to more and more comprehensive view. Variety is the natural recipe for evolution. Rule of law, co-operation and friendly disposition from conviction as well as global policy are all the controls that will suffice.

Values are widely accepted if they promote self esteem, stability and prosperity. Honesty and promise keeping are examples. Corruption can be overcome by values of honesty, efficiency, promptness and transparency in the dealings. The whole of Ramayana is around the value of promise keeping by Dashrath and Rama. Countless sacrifices have been made by women of the world, the Rajputs, the Sikh Gurus and many other cherished heroes and heroines for the value prized by them. Guru Nanak preached practical, simple and humanist way of life devoid of rituals and magic. Love of fellow human beings and love of God was the guiding spirit. Gandhi was the architect of a new value system in India that helped them in their successful struggle for freedom from colonial empire. The value system in science and technology also are parallel to the value system in ethics. Scientific theories are tentative and keep the chase on, of the ever expanding frontiers of knowledge. Social merit is an external criterion of value. Often the social merit shows inertia and is wrongly thwarting a true value and eventually the social merit changes its hue.

Secularism is the glue that binds a complex society. Secularism is the essential quality of God and Nature of acceptance of variety and permitting all things to flourish. Moral values need not be founded on theological dogma. They fulfil present needs and social demands through logic and justice. Historically, secularism stands for education being free from bias towards any particular religious label but secularism is not aversion to religion and a secularist hopes for further advance in all religions and that they could accept scientific advances. Secular outlook stands for inter-personal relations being based on ethics and on mutual interest and not on mutual religious labels. Jawaharlal Nehru called the Indian state secular when the subcontinent was in the throes of the two nation theory and communal hatred. The highest virue is to look at all beings in kinship and to alleviate the pain of others. There is need to build a world of common society. A commitment to peace is necessary for continuous progress in the evolving social environment. Treating others as own self is the highest wisdom. There is an oft repeated prayer that looks at everyone as a good man of culture.

The Roman emperor Mark Aurelius, an arch secularist, declared the brotherhood of man and the moral unity of mankind. Dewey, an American philosopher, declared that the morals are closest to human nature. The Hindus regard the ancient Hinduism to be nothing but humanism. A responsible society matches its rewards and admiration to the moral action displayed. People feel revulsion from fanaticism of all kinds. A secularist is pledged to human welfare and human rights for all. All saints have been opposed to ritualism. The progress of secularism will go hand in hand with the scientific approach. The secular approach is necessary for the future world society.

The worship of idols, tombs, trees, snakes will have a respected place. Any disrespect or disparagement of a sacred object or symbol would be an offence against humanity and will deserve a reprimand. All religions and philosophies including communism and atheism constitute pillars of society.

An important aspect of modern life is the programmes radiated by radio and television. Radio reaches out to more people. Radio transmission licenses should be freely given. This will strengthen democracy and enlightenment everywhere. Government and private resources should foot the entire bill. A separate channel can give only news or only advertisements. People would then have the availability of programmes and channels of their interest. In the USA, there are certain channels which do not accept advertisements. Such channels receive money only from listeners. The government funds could come from their budget for education. The continuation of the programmes will depend on the quality as assessed by an independent cultural apex body democratically appointed by the government in consultation with NGO's.

13

UNITED HUMANITY AND GLOBALIZATION

The ideal of a united humanity and globalization is contained in the adage that all humanity is a single family with the motto popularized by Dumas Alexander that all act for each and each acts for all. The ideal way for lasting unity is unity in diversity. The global mustopia will be formed keeping in mind the policy of acceptance, discussion and co-existence. Continuous advance in science and technology and all embracing education and training will enable every nation to develop in collaboration with others. The current globalization is an exercise in market expansion to reach everyone. So far markets were isolated for a single village or town hemmed in by checks and taxes of all kind. The turnover was small and the purchasing power of the people was dependent on savings of the family which were also marginal. Public was not yet so much used to spending from loans to be paid by future earnings. Easy loans are the key to more production and more earnings, which is the motive power for globalization. International investments in a peace climate further increase the means of communication, growth of infrastructure, better living, and more trade and more profits. The subsistence shopkeeping is giving way to chains of stores, shopping malls and home deliveries on phone call. Super markets are becoming common place. Multinational corporations are entering all business and profit making activities. Large corporations are running coaching institutes and electronic programmes for teaching kids. Migration of workers is becoming simpler and the migrants do not face the ire of locals but are made welcome as wheels that turn on the economics of the host country. Multinationals have set up godowns in supplier countries to make bulk purchases and they also set up production factories with the collaboration of local industrialists. Multinationals are now accepted as means of transfer for capital and knowhow. The banks, financial institutions, traders and entrepreneurs benefit. This globalization has to be coupled to humanist economics so that particular attention is paid to jobs for everyone and elimination of slums and pockets of poverty in the land dotted with extravagance and glittering parties or gaudy entertainment. Taxation and charities will also transfer resources from well-to-do to the needy. A universal maintenance stipend will be available for all citizens of the world whatever their age, community, nationality or sex and the able bodied among the recipients will be required to put in constructive work for about eight hours per week in the service of others. Wealth will be counted in terms of education, skill, means of production and opportunities for recreation and indulging in one's hobbies i.e., in the richness of life and not simply in the money in one's name. The global mustopia will be run as Ram Rajya of the dreams of Gandhi. The idealists as well as the pragmatists and all those who adopt work culture will find fulfilment.

The rise in standard of life will not be dissipated through usual decay and laziness. There will be continuous revolution in improving the mind of individuals as well as the masses. The victory of mind over matters will be the objective of the new struggle, there will be further attempts to control weather over large habitations. There is always scope of improvement in communications. There will be a resurgence of theatrical entertainment and holographic shows. Youth will be attracted to adventure sports. Health and happiness will be added to human rights. Care has to be taken that administration and services are efficient. There is less scope of emergence of corruption in the climate of efficiency and redundancy. Individuals prone to self-aggrandizement would be sidelined to management of zoos and laundries etc. unlike the present practice of sidelining ones who are brilliant but lack humility before authority. A police force will still be employed for maintenance of internal order. It will be the first bulwark against calamities and destruction on account of natural disasters. UN and its Security Council will maintain international order and peace over international highways of commerce. A global order has to pursue universalism that is unity in diversity and a commitment to peace and cooperation. A person placed in authority should be partial to simple against ostentatious living. Consumer complaints would receive prompt attention first through proper training of employees and officials and also through consumer dispute forums with powers to impose and collect fines. The authorities will have many lines of communication bordering on redundancy with the people. Good government needs employees and officials with impeccable personal character and having a value system supported by the community ethos. Secular outlook will have to be taught and emphasized for all. Planning will go for target and timeframes along with the provision of the required resources of men and materials. Creative project work will involve choice and training in new techniques and technologies. System concepts and ultimate analysis will be employed that tries to estimate fall out of any harm to environment and quality of life in the project space and time. The new Mahayana is the philosophy of acceptance and of co-existence. Right action and pragmatism will be the paradigm of the future. Neither the market nor the socialist controls can be made a fetish at the cost of sum total of human happiness. Regional co-operation for peace and security may be of good assistance to the peace keeping efforts of the UN. United action alone will smother terrorism and the peddling of narcotics which are poison for mankind's progress.

Now is the struggle on for a humanist globalization and making the whole world a single family. It would be necessary to diligently and gradually train the next generations in treating others as if they are treating themselves. Once people start feeling the pain of others, the world will be progressing as a single soul. There may be certain weeds in our crop of healthy fruits of civilization which will have to be sidelined as nature does to its many failed species. Quarantine like reservation may have to be created for them to live out their lives. Like people of isolated Easter Island, they may also leave some works depicting their creativity outside the main stream adding to the record of experience of mankind. The direct and indirect co-operation of all nations in many pursuits will bring them closer in a relationship of trust and faith. Development will now mean the actualization of the human potential in everyone. There will be less tension, more income, longer life, and an environment of democracy and equal rights as well as facilities of civilized living for all. Social system will be self corrective. Who can and does help others more, will alone be the basis of self-esteem and social prestige. Determination of social prestige by the position in pecking order will be a dim memory of the infancy of civilization like violence and injustice. Psychiatrists and psychologists will be treating these traits as throwbacks in human nature. UNDP explicitly links human development with human society. All kinds of conflicts can easily be resolved given vigilance and feedback control manipulation. Humanism being naturalism is the practical religion without the super position of deities. Human reason and experience guarantee reliable knowledge which will oust superstition and hankering after miracles and unearned profit. There would be a synthesis of the French, the Russian and the Indian revolutions in the humanization of material and spiritual welfare.

The global culture in its maturity in another five millennia will rest on humanism, secularism and scientific approach. Happiness that can be had would be there for everyone. Participation in festivals and leisure travel for enjoyment will be common and convenient. Such activities in groups can be even more rewarding. Happiness comes from many things, firstly, from satisfaction in one's job or profession. Secularism and the New Mahayana which is an all inclusive mentalism will spread this happiness all around with whomsoever one may interact. The New Mahayana is the pragmatic paradigm of the future world. It does not deny variety and diversity but encompasses them. Our human future is with building this one world and banishing strife and violence by immediate justice and love. The safety valve of redressal of complaints in all dealings will be easy and quick. Gandhi's spirituality and common sense, proper interpretation of Islam, the religion of peace, Christianity, the religion of love and trust, Hindu-Buddhism, the philosophy of right action and belief in cause and effect, merging of new capitalism and socialism give meaning to Indian secularism, mixed economy and the new Mahayana. The world is ready now to move on to humanist economy and the humanist interpretation of history. There is now the opportunity to discover new symbols of cultural integration and co-existence. In the humanist globalization, MNC's will be engaged in reaching merchandise and knowledge, new discoveries, new patents for absorption and use in every nook of the world. Practical democracy means enlightened consensus and assurance of human rights of all.

The current globalization of markets benefits banks, trading entrepreneurs, etc. It will not automatically lead to humanist economics and humanist distribution. The current globalization is only the peak of capitalist distribution. The planners have to transform it to true globalization when pockets of indigence and neglect do not persist. Avenues of charity and parity of wages and compensation for needs of retraining and new production, in countries where imports might make costly production of some kind meaningless, should be made a part of the current globalization of the market.

The globalization of markets means ready availability of merchandise, flow of funds, inputs of knowhow providing efficient production and distribution. Each nation has to cut down its protective tariff so that there is free flow of trade. The nations will not be expected to lower import tariff, on the one hand, and place legal hurdles on imports on the other. This has been attempted by some rich countries specially in the import of drugs and medicines. The cost of production of medicines is prohibitive in Western Europe and USA. This cost is reduced to about one-tenth in India or China. But the USA insist on its food and drug administration's clearance for new drugs specially certain life saving drugs of modern medicine. Alternative medicines are not cleared by US authorities. For example, it is propagated by them that many Indian preparations have heavy elements in objectionable measure. This kind of criticism without tests on human beings is ridiculous. The Indian special drugs have been in use for thousands of years and modern tests by US will also clear them with further experience. Or for a few select drugs joint clinical tests on human being should be carried out to see the worth of such drugs. The heavy metals when used compounded with miscellaneous herbs are not the same compounds as produced by modern synthetic chemistry laboratories.

The low cost drugs from China and India are a boon for humanity. To deny them to populations who need them is nothing but cruelty to people. Some countries will surely come out of this obstruction by creating new laws of their nations advising disregard of food and drug authority of USA etc. The problem of shortage of trained scientists and others in rich countries is forcing them to export jobs. For a united world this should not be regarded as a problem but should be welcome as an equalizer of sorts. The additional training and expertise if available in a less developed country should be utilized to the full and the training institutes there should be utilized for necessary training of own citizens by other countries.

The patent laws and property rights in intellectual products must be such as promote production and more profit to the owners of the rights. In addition, traditional knowledge will not necessarily be patented and it must be regarded as sacred legacy of the whole world. One can, in this connection, cite illegal attempts to patent the cultivation of Basmati rice or use of various parts of the Neem tree. Trade suffers when Shylockian policies are applied.

The working tools of the coming global organization will be nation states co-operating and operating with the apex organizations set up by the UN. The UN system is experimenting with the involvement of democratic activity by inducting NGOs in the UN system of governance.

14

GOVERNANCE

14.1. ROLE OF NATIONAL GOVERNMENTS

National governments are in existence and will be the chief executive for each nation. All nations are going to be members of the UN and the UN expects sincere international co-operation in all measures that go towards peace and progress. Values determine worthwhile goals. Most values have evolved from humanism and ancient heritage. Ignorance, inefficiency, corruption in the administrative apparatus has first to be eliminated. The national governments will get full co-operation from the UN and other nation states in this. Transparency and sincerity in the measures, that are adopted, are most necessary. Democracy does not mean a mechanical roller powered by the legislative majority. Democracy works on the foundation of consensus and trust in the public which wants the nation to prosper and are not to operate an opposition for the sake of opposition. The opposition will always respond to prior discussion and the transparent logic and functioning of the majority. For smooth operations, now the device of opportunity to NGO's for the preparatory discussions can be employed. The media have a responsibility to the national and international interests, and their task of ferreting out the truth, and reaching it to the public and the government is to be respected. Choice of able and honest officials is the basis of good government. The selection of ability is made by all employers and by apex bodies created by the government or by the society for recognizing merit or meritorious service. This selection is very often misused by selfish interests. A court of appeal capable of just dealings must exist where neglected merit can appeal for redress. The methods of an open invitation to oppose the decision for matrimony of a selected bride and groom for marriage is worth attention for all high posts and awards. The views about common honesty and laziness will always be forthcoming in such an event and can help in avoiding a corrupt and dishonest person climbing into a driving seat. The dependence on views of bureaucratic hierarchy should be minimized.

National government is entrusted with internal and external security. With the policy of security of all nations going to be pursued by the UN, the chief concern of the national government is now internal security. In this also the UN will assist in the control of transborder crime, trade in narcotics and misuse of media for cultural pollution. Since it is human to err and often foolish to forgive, a national police and an investigating agency have to be on their toes to successfully meet their objectives. In history, the investigative efficiency has often been allied to wrong objectives like the inquisition, the puritan waves and the ferreting out of fellow travellers in the democracies. This means that public must be kept on the side of law and order by responsible briefing at most stages of the investigation. Moral disorders and anarchy must be suppressed. For security, each nation has to be ready with adequate armed strength to immediately respond to the pockets of rebellion within the country or feeling of insecurity at its international borders. Each nation should be prepared to give assistance within its power to the UN in their onerous duties of international peace keeping and resolution of extended unrest in any country which is also likely to have repercussions in other countries.

The national governments have also to be alive to their responsibility towards the town dwellers and unlike the colonial governments whose primary job was tax collection, law and order, and indifference to the raising of the cultural and economic level of the people. Their idea of non-interference in religious matters allowed the various native religions go downhill under the ministrations of illiterate priests. Their tolerance of ill equipped municipal committees made these the breeding grounds for inefficiency and corruption. Municipal committees and their services must be efficiently run and, if necessary, their work could be handed over to specially trained administrators and ad hoc advisors who were technically qualified to do the allotted job. The realization that inefficiency and corruption persist even in advanced countries is no alibi. In most of the world, the municipal committees are meant to be the training ground for democracy and for work for public good. Now these will also pave the way for humanist policies and for international friendship, peace and progress.

14.2 IMPORTANCE OF THE CURRENT MILLENNIUM

Many a plan for a utopia of peace and prosperity has perished because the success was sought for a small community of likeminded people. We have to take into our calculations for the future of peace and progress of the entire world. There is no paucity of time. Even gradualism adopted by nature in its scheme of evolution will work. Human beings have survived many of the adversities that met other species and man has developed a body of knowledge which is unsurpassed and has only to use it in the interest of all human beings and not for sectarian or sectional benefits which will be self defeating. The world has now reached a period of relative peace and the threat of future wars is receding. If the world makes steady progress in its mental ambitions and the peace and progress continues for one millennium, it is likely to be lasting and mankind can continue to flourish on the earth till eternity. The universalism will come from the aimed unity in diversity. The basic ingredients of humanism, love and non-violence will stand mankind in good stead. The ruler must have many lines of communication with the public even bordering on redundancy.

The UN will have also the function of the chairman of the world governance for welfare, peace and development. The current millennium will be required for considerable effort for education, research, inculcation of democracy, cognizance of human rights and working out of humanist economics and a society of peace and fellow feeling. NGO's will be encouraged to function and contribute to development of international law and make suggestions for improvement.

14.3 GOOD GOVERNMENT

Good government requires fiscal discipline. The public has to earn, save and invest. It must develop the ability to recognize and reward merit. System analysis including the criterion of values has to be adopted i.e., total analysis in place of the engineer's system analysis. It would be in order to study and develop a science of human nature and its dependence on society, training and environment. Ways should be found to confer status and respect on the teachers whose financial income will have to be restricted by the jealous competition by other important vocations for the advancement of human society in all respects. Labour and capital together will build prosperity. Every country should reserve some immigration quota for temporary admission of desired labour or experts. This will diffuse science and technology as well as provide improved prospects to some qualified persons and bring different nations closer. An international traveller will need to carry only his passport as an identification document and proof of financial security for the intended stay abroad. Neither the market nor the socialist controls can be made into an altar at the cost of human happiness.

14.4 GLOBAL GOVERNANCE

Recently a UN panel has recommended the setting up of a peace building commission to work for the internal stability of different nations. A common security system for the entire world is envisaged. The united planning and action will alone meet the challenges of security, terrorism and environmental degradation. The outline of global governance under the aegis of UN is already in place. Inter-governmental conferences have been taking up major concerns off and on, and assigning tasks to some countries and groups who have shown initiative in that direction. It is necessary to accept confirmation from all countries to abide by the protocols concerning weapons of mass destruction. A world body must also be created to combat trans-border and electronic network crimes. A nation state by definition will be one that has enforceable laws within its borders. This automatically ensures laws to have democratic support of its nationals. Within the nation there should be common law and courts must be clear where some relaxation can be allowed even in personal law without creating new complications. Customary law is valid for isolated and backward tribes, but they are to be encouraged to join the mainstream of national growth.

14.5 NEW SOCIAL ORDER

The UN system is to become the global system for change to a new social order. Humanity has already experimented with monolithic systems that have deteriorated into dictatorships or civil war. It is now building up a global system gradually along with change in the value system of the people who now should favour friendship of others and would feel the pain of others as their own. The resolutions passed by the UN General Assembly are recommendatory in nature but they reflect the consensus in the world and would in time become binding with the support of nation states or national courts. The Security Council is soon going to, diminish the present importance of exercise of veto preserved for the five permanent members of the Security Council. It is suggested that a Supreme Peace Council of the world be created democratically with outstanding world status individuals who are known supporters of organized peace and world progress. The veto should be exercised only at the behest of the World Peace Council. A separate UN Economic and Social Council could also be created which will provide administrative assistance and co-ordination to the WTO, IMF, UNDP and WHO than let these work in isolation and sometimes under overlapping responsibility. Various agencies now looking after some world wide programmes will continue with more transparent procedures of selection of programmes and personnel and cut expenses, particularly for the perks and allowances which should not make them some kind of sacred objects to the majority of world population. Certain nations in their pride have reduced the status of the UN by unilaterally attacking Iraq when UN observers were about to give a clean chit to that country on the specific charge of amassing weapons of mass destruction. The world is taking note that similar charges are being thrown at North Korea and Iran.

14.6 POVERTY ALLEVIATION

The world governance is very complex. It has chance of success because of the introduction of computers and new revolution in education and economics. Every voter will have an ID Card and he will be listed along with his address and date of birth in a national computer data storage which is continuously updated because of new persons reaching the voting age and the action of the reaper. The option of some of not accepting the poverty alleviation dole and related required constructive work for eight hours per week will be entered. This listing will be the basis for all municipal, state and national level elections and the disbursement of the poverty alleviation work.

14.7. RULE OF LAW

The rule of law is the best insurance against derailment of democracy. The law courts have become proactive in India, but are failing to have the of capacity to deal with cases promptly with lawyers out to make more money by dragging cases and repeatedly asking for postponement of hearings. The rules of law courts need amendment to remove this delaying mode. The new policy of allowing NGO's to take up matters of policy and gross miscarriage of justice directly in courts as an aggrieved party has been welcomed by most clear thinking people. In reality, the nation state is congruent with the realm of national laws. The law when dealing with backward tribal men and women will give due weight to their customary law and traditions. No tribal slavery or restrictions against civilizational growth of its members as well as children will be tolerated. The views of anthropologists and NGO's, if active in the concerned area, will also be considered. Ordinary citizens will have a common personal law with clear-cut liberties from the law allowed to certain categories. The justice must be quick and, if necessary, special courts could be constituted with minimum red tape to judge similar infringements if coming up too often. Reduction of red tape has been achieved by complaint redressal forums.

Law of inheritance should be examined to weed out incompetent heirs becoming sole arbiters of production apparatus which they might possess as a part of their inheritance. Such properties should be taken up by the government as a trust in the interest of workers, family of the heir and the welfare of the public. Corruption and misdeeds of taxation officials are well known throughout the world. This should cease in democratic free countries with assured human rights. It has not yet ceased perhaps everywhere and the governments are on test in this regard.

Thoreau was the first to use the phrase human rights. Tilak was the first to define freedom as a human right. For self elevation, a man or a society has to transcend lust for material wealth or political power or atleast one of them. Justice is the prime motivation of social institutions.

Equality and freedom are both necessary for peace and progress. Certain religions consider entry by a person of another religion in their temple as a desecration. (Secularism does not look down on someone just because he/she subscribes to another religion). All must be equally welcome in any place of worship so long as they subscribe to the simple discipline expected from a visitor. If the visitor's intentions are confrontation and violence, he is a criminal in the eyes of law when respect of all religions is enjoined. In case, the public is confronted by a group of fanatics committed to indulge in suicide attack on the sacred place, they must be stopped in their tracks. They will seek deliverance only through a court of law. Photography by visitors and pilgrims should be allowed unless it is considered harmful by conservationists. Certain temples in India welcome visitors and tourists but insist that there should be no photographs of their gods and sacred precincts ! New technology can recreate holograms outside the temple precincts.

15

ALERT HUMANITY AND MUSTOPIA MILESTONES

Given below are some milestones regarding the establishment of "Mustopia" in the world. The people may watch the performance of the governance and of mankind against these milestones and take appropriate feedback control adjustments. Mustopia is another version of Oughtopia proposed in 1983 by seek Choue of Korea. It is the mother of all utopias proposed in human history. The major difference is that it must happen and it is not just a trial balloon for satisfaction of a coterie. The people of the world should be conscious that with energetic action and perpetual alertness, mankind has to live on this earth for a minimum of two billion years more. They can do so since the foundation of Mustopia are already laid and the initial favourable conditions are now occurring. Humanity could build on the outlines given in detail in this book. The UN has to be given more co-operation and UN system of governance expanded with nation states staying put as the UN reps and free agents for the conversion of their nations to Mustopia standards. They have to re-construct their nations into paths of peace and friendship, educate them and provide adequate training, create wealth and values which are necessary to eradicate poverty in one sweep, and channel all charity through decentralized district level. A humanist economics is sure to be a success. The UN and the nations together will assure security for all, both internal and external. It will be a multipolar world, with each nation acting as a pole upholding rule of law and pursuing a secular approach based on universal ethics. Setting up of an Economic Security Council is endorsed along with a World Peace Council with whose approval alone any measure required by the General Assembly can be vetoed down. Whole mankind is invited to welcome advances in human health, mental abilities and the unification of the world based on faith and reason acting together for the benefit of mankind. The Mustopia will be reached by each nation at its own speed following its own strategy. Time available is in plenty.

Milestone	Flow of Time
Effective Start of human civilization (Hammarabi and the Vedas, Egyptian and Chinese empires)	3000 B.C.
The Buddha, Cofucius, Greek bloom.	6th and 7th centuries B.C.
Christ	0-33 A.D.
Start of Science, Islam, Regeneration of Hinduism	7th and 8th centuries A.D.
Beginning of the modern age (Discovery of America, Charting of lands and oceans by European sailors and explorers)	15th and 16th centuries A.D.
World organized as nation states without ethical discipline and perpetual Anarchy plus contribution of many men of genius: Lincoln, Napoleon, Darwin, Marx, Nehru, Einstein, Gandhi	2nd millennium
Beginning of post-modern period in 1948 when (UN was established), Consolidation of UN system of management of internal and external peace,	3rd millennium

Milestone	Flow of Time
National effort in each country for education, humanist economics and eradication of poverty, advance in biology and nano-materials, long life and good health of all.	4th millennium

Applied Biology, cybernetics, astronomy, and advances in DNA manipulation. Steady progress in arts of civilized life and social and in DNA material.

...Remaining eternity

GLOSSARY AND NOTES

Bhakti : Prayers and devotion to a chosen God. A religion of peace and love.

Bhrigu: A Hindu seer of antiquity. Besides codifying rules of conduct and praising humility, he gave predictions about whole mankind including those who were yet to be born.

Chreod: A stable trajectory of development.

Eukaryotic Cell: A living cell using genetic code leading to multi-cellular life. On the other hand, a prokaryotic cell is the single cell life which multiplied by division of one cell into two and was abundant before the earth got oxygen in the atmosphere.

Feynman, Prof. R.P. (1918–1988): A renouned Nobel laureate professor of Physics and teacher who advocated teaching by exciting curiosity among the students and then guiding them in their efforts to satisfy their curiosity. He invented the Feynman diagrams of Quantum Theory.

Genome: Human genome has 23 chromosomes on which are situated 30,000 to 60,000 genes. Each cell in the body contains a nucleus made of two complete sets of genomes. There are small differences in the maternal and paternal version of each genome.

Guru: A teacher and guide for holy life.

Maslo Needs: Maslo defined human needs as physical security, status, autonomy, self-actualization; Prof. Indiresan has added ecological need to the list.

Micro-chip: A specially prepared piece of a semi-conductor usually silicon used as an element in electrical or optical circuits. The use of such chips has reduced the size and price of computer and all electrical appliances.

Nehru, Jawaharlal (1889–1964): The foremost leader and follower of Mahatma Gandhi in the Indian struggle for freedom. A socialist and secularist. Elected first prime minister of free India. He was the architect of Indian foreign policy of peace and co-existence.

New Mahayana: An extension of Mahayana approach to religion, to both religion and political theory. It admits and approves the co-existence of many gods and many philosophies. It is the essential basis of multi-religious nations and multi-polar world integration into one community.

Ontogenesis: Biological development of an individual from a zygot to old age.

Phylogeny: Evolutionary development of a plant or an animal species.

Purans, Pauranic Fiction: Hindu religious and didactic literature. Usually depicting lives and deeds of gods, goddesses and human heroes of faith.

Saha, M.N. (1893–1956): Physicist who dominated science and planning scene in India. A rationalist and man with a vision.

Sarvodaya: Literally welfare of all. The favourite goal of Mahatma Gandhi for independent India.

Stagflation: Inflation plus stagnation.

Thoreau. H.D. (1817–1862): American philosopher, who believed in ethics as foundations of society. He believed in a life of simplicity, independence, magnanimity and trust.

Tilak, Bal Gangadhar (1856–1920): Indian reformer and political leader who introduced Gandhi to the people of India when Gandhi returned from his successful political experiments and struggle in South Africa against apartheid. He gave the clarion call that freedom is the birth right of all. He popularized the Ganesh festival for national integration.

Vedas: There are four Vedas or Hindu holy books containing knowledge revealed at start of civilization. Most of the foundation holy books predate the Buddha. Hindus revere the Buddha as one of themselves but an atheist since he did not hold the Vedas as final authority and held reason and experience as the touchstone. Modern Hindus hold that religion has to square up with science and technology.

Yoga: The Hindu system of physical and breath control exercises that prolong one's life and open the mind to inner spiritual life.

BIBLIOGRAPHY

Ali. Tariq (1982), *The Clash of Fundamentalisms*, Rupa and Co., Delhi.

Bemildoz, Pedro B. (2002), Young Seek Choue's Thought and Strategies, Aquinas Univ.

B T Bas (1980), *Economic Theory and Ideology*, Edward Arnold.

Ghosh, Benoy Jiwan (1987), *The Clash of Fundamentalism,* Rupa and Co., Delhi.

Bhagwati, Jagadish (2004), *In Defence of Globalization,* Oxford Univ. Press.

Buttin, M.O. (1962), *Geophysica Aspects of Origin of Life*, Elsevier.

Dinkar, D.A. (2004), Challenge for Progress and Peace, *Gandhi Marg*, pp. 133-157.

Dixon, David and N. Rawlia (Ed) (1995), *The New Macroeconomics*, Cambridge Univ. Press.

Durant, Will (1935-1975), *Story of Civilization* (Vol. 1-11), Simon and Schuster.

Fine, Jiwan (1987), *Revolt of 1905 in Bengal*, Ind.Pub. Society, Kolkata.

Grouchear, S.L. (2004), *Globalization and Belonging,* Reiman and Littlefield N.Y.

Handelman, Howard (2000), *The Challenge of the Third World Dev.*, Prentice Hall.

Hodgson, G.M. (1993), *Economics and Evolution*, Polity Press.

Inter. Rev. Edn. (2004), *Globalization and Local Indigenous Education in Mexico.*

Indiresan, P.V. (2003), *Vision 2020,* ICFAI Univ., Chennai.

Laqueur, Walter (2003), *No End to War, Terrorism in the 21st Century*, Continuum NY.

Lasky, Melvin J. (1976), *Utopia and Revolution*, Univ. Chicago Press.

Little, I.M.D. (1950), *A Critique of Welfare Economics*, Oxford Univ. Press.

Nanda, J.N. (1977), *Foreign Policy of Co-existence*, Ashish Verma Pub., Delhi.

Nanda, J.N. (2003), *Religion and Philosophy for Modern Youth*, Concept Publishing Company, New Delhi.

Official Guide Book (1977), U.N., New York.

Ridley, Mat. (2000), *Genome*, Perennial, N.Y.

Stern, Geoffry (2000), *The Structure of International Society,* Pinter., N.Y.

Walker, Kenneth (1954), *Story of Medicine*, Hutchinson, London.

Wheelan L., Charles (2002), *Naked Economics*, Norton and Co. World Science Report (1998), UNESCO.

Zachary, G. Pascal (2000), *The Global Me*, Nicholas Brealey, U.K.

INDEX